BENTON BLACK HAWK BOONE BREMER

RROLL CASS CEDAR CERRO GORDO CHEROKEE

CRAWFORD DALLAS DAVIS DECATUR DELAWARE

FLOYD FRANKLIN FREMONT GREENE GRUNDY

HENRY HOWARD HUMBOLDT IDA IOWA JACKSON

SUTH LEE LINN LOUISA LUCAS LYON MADISON

MONONA MONROE MONTGOMERY MUSCATINE

POCAHONTAS POLK POTTAWATTAMIE POWESHIEK

A TAYLOR UNION VAN BUREN WAPELLO WARREN

NNESHIEK WOODBURY WORTH WRIGHT ADAIR

TON BLACK HAWK BOONE BREMER BUCHANAN

CEDAR CERRO GORDO CHEROKEE CHICKASAW

DALLAS DAVIS DECATUR DELAWARE DES MOINES

FRANKLIN FREMONT GREENE GRUNDY GUTHRIE

HOWARD HUMBOLDT IDA IOWA JACKSON JASPER

LINN LOUISA LUCAS LYON MADISON MAHASKA

MONROE MONTGOMERY MUSCATINE O'BRIEN

AS POLK POTTAWATTAMIE POWESHIEK RINGGOLD

YLOR UNION VAN BUREN WAPELLO WARREN

WINNESHIEK WOODBURY WORTH WRIGHT

ADAIR ADAMS ALLAMAKEE APPANOOSE AUD

BUCHANAN BUENA VISTA BUTLER CALHOUN C

CHICKASAW CLARKE CLAY CLAYTON CLINTON

DES MOINES DICKINSON DUBUQUE EMMET FAYE

GUTHRIE HAMILTON HANCOCK HARDIN HARRISO

JASPER JEFFERSON JOHNSON JONES KEOKUK KO

MAHASKA MARION MARSHALL MILLS MITCHELL

O'BRIEN OSCEOLA PAGE PALO ALTO PLYMOUTH

RINGGOLD SAC SCOTT SHELBY SIOUX STORY TA

WASHINGTON WAYNE WEBSTER WINNEBAGO W

ADAMS ALLAMAKEE APPANOOSE AUDUBON BE

BUENA VISTA BUTLER CALHOUN CARROLL CAS

CLARKE CLAY CLAYTON CLINTON CRAWFORD

DICKINSON DUBUQUE EMMET FAYETTE FLOYD

HAMILTON HANCOCK HARDIN HARRISON HENRY

JEFFERSON JOHNSON JONES KEOKUK KOSSUTH L

MARION MARSHALL MILLS MITCHELL MONON

OSCEOLA PAGE PALO ALTO PLYMOUTH POCAHON

SAC SCOTT SHELBY SIOUX STORY TAMA

WASHINGTON WAYNE WEBSTER WINNEBAGO

O

IOWA

A Celebration of Land, People & Purpose

IOWA

15⊙

Celebrate
Our State

1 8 4 6 ✿ 1 9 9 6

© 1993, Iowa Sesquicentennial Commission, Inc.

The Official Commemorative Book of the Iowa Sesquicentennial

© Copyright 1995, Iowa Sesquicentennial Commission. All rights reserved. Printed in the U.S.A.

Produced by Meredith Publishing Services, 1912 Grand Avenue, Des Moines, IA 50309-3379.

First Edition. Library of Congress Catalog Card Number: 95-78093

ISBN: 0-696-20518-1

IOWA SESQUICENTENNIAL COMMISSION

CHAIRMAN
HON. ROBERT D. RAY
Des Moines

CO-CHAIR
C.J. NILES
Carroll

C. JOSEPH COLEMAN
Clare

DAVID CROSSON
Brooklyn

FRANK J. DELANEY III
Burlington

CHALMERS "BUMP" ELLIOTT
Iowa City

ALMO HAWKINS
Des Moines

MARILYN CARTER
Sioux City

MARY MASCHER
Iowa City

MARILYN McDONALD
Dubuque

ANNE E. NELSON
Council Bluffs

DAVID T. NELSON
Decorah

JOHN NELSON
Estherville

EDWARD C. NICHOLS
Knoxville

REBECCA REYNOLDS-KNIGHT
Keosauqua

SUE RICHTER
Milford

WILLIAM ROBA
Davenport

LUKE ROTH
Des Moines

EMILY A. RUSSELL
Oskaloosa

JANE SEATON
Corning

DONN STANLEY
Des Moines

ROSE VASQUEZ
Des Moines

DONALD W. WANATEE, SR.
Tama

PEGGY WHITWORTH
Cedar Rapids

JUNEAN G. WITHAM
Cedar Falls

PUBLISHED FOR THE
IOWA SESQUICENTENNIAL
COMMISSION BY MEREDITH
PUBLISHING SERVICES

AUTHORS
Hugh Sidey
Cornelia F. Mutel
Mary Swander
Craig Canine
Michael Martone

EDITOR
Pamela Johnson

CONTRIBUTING EDITORS
Craig Canine
Hugh Sidey

ART DIRECTOR
Brian Shearer

DESIGNERS
Chris Conyers
Brett Rooks
Stacy Lautzenheiser

PHOTOGRAPHY RESEARCH
Virginia Wadsley

PUBLISHER
Michael Peterson

MARKETING DIRECTOR
Brad Elmitt

PRODUCTION MANAGER
Rick von Holdt

PHOTOGRAPHY
This book would not have been possible without the creative contributions of many photographers. They are identified and credited on page 192, as are individuals and institutions who provided archival photos for this project. Subjects, dates, and locations appear with all photographs for which such information was available. Contemporary, non-dated images are mostly from the 1980s and '90s.

*T*hrough fickle winds of blizzards and heat, floods and drought, Iowans have emerged a unique people. A people who steward the land and feed the world; a people who love God and help their neighbors; a people who understand their place in the world and have the most uncommon common sense.

We are first and foremost good people. We believe in hard work, honesty, and commitment to public service. We know that the education of our children is the ticket to our future, and from the one-room township schoolhouse to the fiber optic network, we have never doubted our faith in education.

Whether we live in city or country, apartment or farmhouse, we are not far from the land. Our values are grounded in the deep black earth that covers this state.

We are people committed to quality. The productivity and skill of our workers in Iowa gets the job done right, the first time.

The Sesquicentennial offers Iowa the perfect opportunity to reflect on our proud history, plan for a bright future, and most importantly, celebrate who we are—a state of neighbors and families and small communities.

Governor Terry E. Branstad

Blue Cross and Blue Shield of Iowa has been dedicated to the health and well being of Iowans for almost 60 years. We are proud to be a partner with the Iowa Sesquicentennial Commission for the publication of this official commemorative book.

Blue Cross/Blue Shield
Corporate Partner

IOWA SESQUICENTENNIAL ADMINISTRATIVE TEAM

J. Scott Raecker
Executive Director

Mary Ann Ubiñas
Associate Director

Meg Courter
Project Manager

Paulette Ihrig
Administrative Assistant

Kay A. Swan
Field Representative, Central Region

Becky Swanson
Field Representative, Eastern Region

Jane Nielsen
Field Representative, Western Region

Amelia Morris
Public Relations Director

Anna Conradt
Receptionist/Secretary

Rachelle H. Saltzman, Ph.D.
Iowa Folklife Coordinator

Bonnie Jacob
Project Consultant, Blue Cross/Blue Shield

Anniversaries, by definition, occur every year. Most pass with barely a nod. Some anniversaries, though, we recognize as mileposts. They give us occasion to pause, measure how far we have come, and peer into the possibilities of the future. Iowa's Sesquicentennial in 1996 marks the 150th year of our statehood. Iowans

have always thought of our home as a quiet place, where changes, like the seasons, move at their leisure. Now, from the vantage point of this landmark year, we see clearly that our accumulated progress has been breathtaking. In 1846, when Iowa became the 29th state, we were a society of immigrant pioneers, staking our hopes on a stark, demanding prairie. By our 1896 Golden Jubilee, we had sown the seeds of our destiny not only as a farming state, but as a heartland center for industry and trade. At our Centennial in 1946, we celebrated the end of World War II and the beginning of an era of growth and creativity that would bring Iowa to a place of prominence in our nation and abroad. Today, the products of our fields feed the world and the products of our manufacturing plants are staples in countless homes, farms, and businesses. Iowa-built systems provided the communications links that let billions watch and listen as Apollo 11 took the first earthlings to the moon. Iowa men and women, products of our renowned educational system, have always been among our nation's great innovators, artists, humanitarians, leaders, and doers. This book is dedicated to all those pioneers who came—and continue to come—to make their homes in our beautiful state. Gathered at this Sesquicentennial milepost, we look forward to tomorrow, as unbounded as our vision and as free as our dreams.

The Honorable Robert D. Ray
Chairman,
Iowa Sesquicentennial Commission

TABLE OF CONTENTS

"The deep black earth and vaulted sky speak Iowa's language. It is
a language of patience and common sense and joy in hard work. It
is, after 150 years of settling and learning, a language of enlightened progress and renewal."

"Land of green and brown, of life and earth, of rivers and sky, of
grasses waving in the breeze. Land of hybrid grasses, or cornfields,
of yellowing kernels encased in drying husks etched against the hot
blue sky. Iowa: for many thousands of years, a land of grasses."

"By all rights, we should be a bland and loosely affiliated group.
But anyone who moves here quickly comes to see that the people of
Iowa have an unusual sense of self-identity."

"The last 150 years have seen a robust flowering of human
enterprise on Iowa soil—farms, schools, industries, cities, towns,
places of worship, recreational opportunities, the arts. While none
of these expressions of culture is unique to Iowa, there is a coherence here, a unifying core of values that provides the state with its
own singular sense of purpose and energy."

"Iowans, it seems to me, are particularly adept at negotiating the
meeting of the past and future, at negotiating the transformations of
yesterdays into tomorrows."

"Is this heaven?"
"No, it's Iowa."
Twilight scene
in Johnston,
Polk County

INTRODUCTION: IOWA'S LANGUAGE

By Hugh Sidey

The psalm from the movie *Field of Dreams*—"Is this heaven? No, It's Iowa"—has taken its place in the sound-bite firmament, but its lilt is as old and true as the land. On first viewing Iowa in 1804, Captain Meriwether Lewis described what he saw as "the most beautiful prospect." Thirty years later, the Reverend Era Hyde would call it "glorious, broad, free, soul-kindling country." And today, Dan Offenberger of Shenandoah says, "I am convinced that Iowa is now one of the most livable places on earth." I confess prejudice as a person born and reared in Iowa. Yet, in living beyond its borders and returning eagerly and often, I have scrutinized Iowa as part of a continental mosaic of people and land. It is truly a special place. There is harmony and ample elbow room and a human proportion that has been squandered in so many other areas in the nation. Iowa has a subtle magic that was God-given at first, but has been protected and enlarged by Iowa's generations and now yields a culture that has remarkable virtues. So often in my long journeys, Iowa has floated up as a touchstone for food production, good kids and common sense. "You like coming back?" Senator John Kennedy once asked me as we bumped through the spring air on board the *Caroline* in his quest for the presidency. He was looking down at the vivid land-quilt as we crossed the Mississippi River and lowered toward Cedar Rapids.

MIST ON THE
PASTURE NEAR
HARTFORD,
WARREN COUNTY

FARMER AND
GRANDSON NEAR
NORTH LIBERTY,
JOHNSON COUNTY,
1946

IA
—
10

"Sure," I answered. "It is home. You have to understand the prairie."

I recall that he bobbed his head and grinned. He liked that. He was intrigued by the unfamiliar, by the hint of adventure. For a few long seconds, he was silent, staring at the rich greens and blacks filling the cabin window. "My world is beaches and oceans," he said. "But I always remember something Robert Frost said: 'It's a shame to grow crops and run them through animals for food, because that black Iowa soil looks good enough to eat as it is.'"

That tempting black Iowa soil, a full quarter of all the nation's prime farmland, has yielded much more than grain (which, when all is said and done, may be the lesser product). That soil has produced a rare and

seamless community that is state-wide—a people woven together by shared concerns and disciplines who remain bound to the exciting and dazzling cycles of nature, yet schooled, capitalized and equipped for the global village and the information highway.

After the disturbing summit between Kennedy and Nikita Khrushchev in Vienna in 1961, I asked the President for his personal assessment of the Soviet boss. He waved my question aside with a grimace and said, "Your damned Iowans are about the only people he seems to respect. Nothing seems to bother him but the fear that he can't feed his people. If he ever invaded the U.S., I think he would head straight for Iowa."

When I was among an adventuresome band of Americans who arrived in China with Richard Nixon in 1972, about the only solid

link with the West that I saw there was some pamphlets on farming from Iowa State University, neatly preserved in a rack at a state farm.

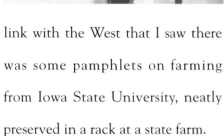

Once in Moscow when I was introduced to Leonid Brezhnev, he looked monumentally bored with my credentials until Nixon explained that I hailed from Iowa. Brezhnev's heavy lids shot up, and he actually smiled. "Good place," he said. "Lots of corn and hogs." Mikhail Gorbachev had the same reaction years later in the White House at one of those noisy, milling receptions. "I know about Iowa," said Gorbachev, who once was the political overseer of Soviet agriculture. "I respect and admire what they do."

Coffee time at a
local repair shop,
Ringgold County

Children of
Hispanic migrant
workers at school
in Muscatine,
Muscatine County,
early 1960s

NIKITA KHRUSHCHEV
AND ROSWELL GARST
AT A RECEPTION
WELCOMING THE
SOVIET LEADER TO
IOWA, 1958

LUNCHTIME AT NOLLEN
PLAZA, DOWNTOWN
DES MOINES,
POLK COUNTY

When national attention began to focus on Iowa because of its early presidential caucuses, I lost track of the number of my colleagues who came back well chilled from the winter winds but fascinated by the pervasive human warmth and the high degree of understanding among the people about what was at stake. At a seminar at Yale one time, I found myself with one of the faculty members who screened student applications. Who would get the coveted acceptances, I asked. Without hesitation, the man responded that a boy or a girl from Iowa who stood near the top of the class and had been a leader in his church or community was an almost

certain winner. "It is remarkable," he said, "year after year, how those kids out there lead in the testing and have so much character."

After the terrible floods of 1993, NBC anchorman Tom Brokaw, who had produced some of his nightly shows from Iowa during the crisis, grabbed my arm. "You'd have been proud of those Iowans," he told me. "They were just magnificent, helping each other, giving to each other."

Providence did not simply select a special group of people and put them down in some primordial lottery on that garden spot between the great rivers. President Thomas Jefferson bought the 36 million acres of Iowa, along with a lot of lesser territory in

the Louisiana Purchase, for about four cents an acre. Few people, if any, really understood that the area was the world's greatest renewable resource, a haven of wealth beyond reckoning. But, to those who had the heart to breast the vastness of the prairie and the mind to listen and learn, that land formed a base that, in the words of author John Madson, was "a repository of traditional attitudes that are metered out through the root system in subtle but powerful ways. It is a region whose soil base has lent the freedom and stability that men need to reach free and stable conclusions."

Stable and even—always that. The wealth of soil had been ladled out generously from border to border.

ARCHITECTS AT A
BUILDING SITE,
CHARTING IOWA'S
GROWTH

The rain with heavenly regularity brushed the hills and swales. The extremes of cold and heat were subdued. God seemed to cradle the land in His hand and make it the taproot of this republic. Every part of Iowa was equally good, and people spread themselves evenly across the abundance. Communities, schools and churches followed in logical patterns. Then roads and railroads, uninhibited by mountains and forests, were rushed across the gentle swells, scratching squares between the fields. No big cities grew up, just towns, small and big, and then bigger.

Those half-dozen truly urban areas are, in reality, loose confederations of neighborhoods and towns benignly stitching together office buildings, universities, shopping malls and service centers. Traffic jams are rarely worthy of the name. But the enterprises—insurance, publishing, and transportation, to name a few—are of national stature.

The deep black earth and vaulted sky speak Iowa's language. It can be heard in the harmony of seasons by those who are born and live here, and is carried forever by those who wander. It is a language of patience and common sense and joy in hard work. It is the language of achievement, of growing corn and soybeans and hogs and cattle beyond imagining. It is, after 150 years of settling and learning, a language of enlightened progress and renewal.

Iowa whispered to me when I was a young boy growing up in Greenfield. Stories were told at the family table of Great-grandfather riding the railroad as far as it went, then striding off over unmarked prairie to find a home and found a livelihood. I listened to those blizzards when the snow blew parallel to the ground and shrieked their warnings, only partly heeded by bundled, laughing kids. I listened to the soft spring air when gardening was a ritual of family love, with the sigh of earth being newly turned, of robins scolding, and of twilight suppers with Mother and Father beneath fragrant lilacs.

A BIRD'S-EYE VIEW
OF ELDORADO,
FAYETTE COUNTY

I read Iowa's language in literature and in history books—stories of early farmers marveling because they plowed up more birds' nests than stones, of the terrible beauty of sun and infinite horizon that drove the timid back into the forests but revealed its marvelous secrets to the wise and strong, of Henry A. Wallace out of the soil of my own county, of hybrid grains and animals and new machines and fertilizers that produced enough food to fuel a nation and a world that stood in awe of Iowa's achievement.

I heard the language of Iowa in a church basement with threshing crews eating a mountain of potatoes and a ton of pot roast. And I listened to Iowa laughter, as ceaseless as the prairie wind—life-sustaining laughter in the depths of drought and depression, laughter from a twinkle-eyed farmer whose only wealth was his wit. Know how to get rid of grasshoppers? Take two lengths of two-by-four, catch a hopper, put it on one board and slam the other one down on the insect. Just keep it up until they're all gone.

Iowa's language now is heard in the whir of factories, an accompaniment to the eternal rustling, ripening grain. It is now fitted to better education, higher skills, new products and services, and distant markets. It speaks through fiber-optic cables that run through the ancient valleys of

Sunset at planting
time near Readlyn,
Bremer County

THE DES MOINES
RIVER AND CAPITAL-CITY
SKYLINE AT TWILIGHT,
POLK COUNTY

the Nodaway and Wapsipinicon rivers. It tells of an urban-rural alchemy of well-being that is unequaled in any other state. Factories and laboratories in low profile have taken up residence in the vast expanses of grain, for the most part quiet, uncomplaining and industrious neighbors in productivity. Russia's Aeroflot planes use a collision-avoidance system made in Iowa, the Disney empire uses software from the state, and Manhattan cloaks some of its skyscrapers with sheets of Iowa-made insulated glass. The sheets roll out on trucks night and day along the great highways that feed into the other states, most of them less than two days' drive away.

Today in Iowa there are about 100,000 businesses, tiny and large, scattered among 100,000 farms, which themselves have become businesses with management techniques matching those of the banks and insurance firms and supply companies that serve agriculture. There are a thousand cities and towns, many of them now reshaping themselves for a new wave of Iowa culture.

No Iowa farmer now lives more than 25 miles from a hospital. There is no high-school student who cannot try his or her hand at basketball or French. And there is no Iowan anywhere in the state who is more than 20 minutes from the sublime call of a meadowlark.

A RICH,
GENTLE & WATERED LAND

By Cornelia F. Mutel

IOWA: it means beautiful land. A land whose beauty lies in her natural wealth. Land of green and brown, of life and earth, of rivers and sky, of grasses waving in the breeze. Land of hybrid grasses, of cornfields, of yellowing kernels encased in drying husks etched against the hot blue sky. Iowa: for many thousands of years, a land of grasses. Native peoples knew it thus for thousands of years before European settlement. An ample land of favorable climate, well-watered both from above and under the ground, the land we now call Iowa lay in the heart of the tallgrass prairie, one of Earth's largest and most productive grasslands.

CANADA GOLDENROD
IN TALLGRASS PRAIRIE,
PRAIRIE CREEK
WILDLIFE REFUGE,
MARSHALL COUNTY

A new wave of settlers, wading from eastern forests into the grassland sea in the 1800s, must have wondered whether they would survive the prairie's sprays of wind, its frothing fires, its wave upon wave of grass blades and seed heads cresting higher than a horse's head, dense enough to hide a herd of cattle. They must have marveled at the color: the golden rays of compass plant and sawtooth sunflower, the rich autumn rusting of big bluestem, the lavender spikes of blazing stars, and the dances of bobolinks. And at the stillness and sound: thunderous herds of bison, wedges of long-billed curlews whistling on the wing, rivers of golden plovers, the calls and cackles of migrants flying through by the millions.

AUTUMN MIGRATION
OF SNOW GEESE,
DE SOTO NATIONAL
WILDLIFE REFUGE,
HARRISON COUNTY

Certainly these new settlers despaired at the marshes, sloughs, and potholes soaking the land. Yet even these yielded life in profusion: clouds of geese, ducks, swans, whooping and sandhill cranes, egrets. Pelican eggs could be collected by the boatload.

It is said that the European settlers first feared this land of limitless grass, wind, sky, and fire, and clung instead to the forests strung through the region alongside the ribbons of rivers and which, toward the moister east, climbed up hillsides: forests of oak and hickory, of maple and basswood, draped each spring in a profusion of hepatica, trillium, rue anemone, spring beauty, and other spring wildflowers, darkened by huge flocks of passenger pigeons, abounding in wild turkey and deer. The settlers clung, as well, to the savannas—flower-speckled parklands that lined the forest's edge and stretched westward along ridgetops. Here a person could ride a horse with ease for miles beneath the spreading limbs of wide-spaced, broad-crowned white and bur oaks, crossed by great herds of elk and by roaming bears and wolves.

WOOD DUCK (TOP);
COMMON EGRET (MIDDLE);
PHEASANT PAIR (BOTTOM);
BUTTERFLY MILKWEED,
BLACK-EYED SUSANS,
AND OX-EYE SUNFLOWERS,
MARSHALL COUNTY
(FACING PAGE)

A SUGAR MAPLE GLOWS
WITH AUTUMN GOLD
NEAR DECORAH,
WINNESHIEK COUNTY

WHITE-TAILED DEER

WHITE-BREASTED
NUTHATCH

Farmer and team
mowing hay,
early 1940s,
Jones County

Euro-Americans settled the wood-lands first, hacking away the trees for heat and shelter. Then they discovered the richness of the grasslands. Directly beneath the bluestem and Indian grass lay Iowa's "black gold," her thick friable topsoil, fed for eons by the prairie's decomposing remains and kneaded by dense root masses of grasses, sunflowers, and legumes stretching five, ten, perhaps twenty feet down to resurrect buried nutrients. They set out to mine these rich prairie-bred soils and transform a heaven of sound and sight into something more tenable by their standards.

PRESENT-DAY
CORNFIELD,
OSCEOLA COUNTY

New tones pierced the prairie air: the thud of oxen hooves, the twang of the plow. Pawing bison and booming prairie chickens, once numbering in the countless thousands, yielded to bawling cattle and baying dogs. Quenched were the raging fires that could outrace a horse, so loved by prairies and savannas but feared by the new settlers. Finally even sloughs and potholes were ditched, tiled, and planted to row crops. Thirty million acres of Iowa prairie, for millennia purified and purged of trees by fire and drought, now were forced to yield their riches without return.

Today the scattered remnants linger here and there: a russet patch of prairie grass alongside a dirt roadway, a brilliant orange cluster of butterfly milkweed near a deserted train track. A flurry of shooting stars purpling a pioneer cemetery, flower-scented clouds of lavender and yellow floating through the few prairie preserves that speckle the state: Steele Prairie and Sheeder, Hayden and Cayler, Freda Haffner Kettlehole, those of the drier Loess Hills. Here and there a lone white oak, round-topped and massive, outlines its savanna reminiscences against the setting sun, or a mature tree grove whispers of the extensive forests that once were. Whirlwinds of glistening snow geese, winging north along the Missouri each March, honk the memories of the countless thousands that once flew here.

BUR OAK TREE
IN A FIELD OF
DRYING CORN,
MONONA COUNTY

Settlers' wagon
passing through
Clinton,
Clinton County,
mid-1800s

Perhaps the settlers who first pierced this land peered into the past and sensed that the border between woodland and grassland had always been restless. That whenever the climate warmed and dried, over periods of hundreds or thousands of years, the drought-resistant prairies shoved the forests many hundreds of miles to the east. When the rains returned, the supple oak forests rebounded westward. Perhaps the 19th-century settlers noticed strange, drought-loving remnants of earlier arid periods scattered through Iowa on the very driest sites: ornate box turtles crawling along sandy banks of the Iowa and Cedar rivers, plains pocket mice leaping along the Big Sand Mound near Muscatine. Cowboy's delight and other Great Plains species flourished in the Loess Hills, relicts that remain even today to remind us of the power of the skies and changing climates to shape life on earth.

If the pioneers spreading westward could have gazed even more deeply into the past, they would have seen that this land of prairies once had lain hostage to ice. For more than two million years, glaciers had slowly surged from the Subarctic southward over ancient Iowa, only to ebb when warmth returned, pulsating in tempo with the climate. Smoothing the land with a harsh frozen mitt, they had dumped their ground-up leavings of grit and rock in thick blankets and stony ridges. The settlers, facing the winter's northern skies, might in their mind's eye have imagined the frigid air wafting from the glaciers' frozen walls, smelled their moist cold, or heard their thousands of feet of ice ponderously grinding and compressing the land into new shapes. They certainly saw the bolder signs of glacial presence that still mark the landscape today: thick layers of unsorted pebbles, angular rocks,

and other glacial debris that blanket nearly all of Iowa, and sharp-edged boulders, scratched and planed by ice, which speckled farmers' fields and slammed their plows.

Even as the wandering fields of ice smeared the earth flat, winds and waters played upon the land. Each glacial recession released torrents of meltwaters, which carved the broad, flat valleys of the Missouri, Des Moines and Mississippi rivers, and frosted them thickly with fine-textured sediments. Strong winds rising from the glaciers' cold margins scoured the valley floors, lifting their sediments to cloak the state with a softer quilt of silt, called loess. The settlers who later traversed the landscape cursed the difficulties of the deepest loess deposits, the maze of western Iowa's sharp-peaked Loess Hills, where horses struggled to find footing and wagons teetered precariously along bluff edges.

$\dfrac{1}{40}$

Glaciers last covered the entire state a half-million years ago. Since then, the rains have sculpted the raw landscape, etching ever-deeper and more intricate drainage networks. The process continues: today, even though the glaciers and arctic-bred winds slumber, ribbons of water continue to cut through Iowa's thick layers of rock and soil, washing them to the sea.

Patterns on the land:
new houses in
West Des Moines,
Polk County

SIGNS OF AUTUMN ON
IOWA'S LAND QUILT,
DUBUQUE COUNTY

The Mormons, setting out from Nauvoo, Illinois, to forge a major pioneer trail across southern Iowa, crossed the deeply creased billows and swales of this water-carved land, fingered everywhere with drainages. So do today's travelers on Interstate 80.

But not those who drive northern Interstate 35, which transects a broad peninsular tongue stretching south to modern Des Moines. Here, about 14,000 years ago, the glaciers made one final, crunching play. They flattened the hills and drainages, once again flooding the river valleys and feeding them with sand and silt. The glaciers brought in the last load of rocky parent material that would be weathered and nurtured into today's rich soils. After gouging out Spirit Lake, Clear Lake, Lake Okoboji, and thousands of potholes, they melted back a mere 12,000 years ago to leave north-central Iowa's "Des Moines Lobe" a boggy flatland with garlands of hummocky hills. Then, eight or nine thousand years ago, as the land we call Iowa quieted, as the last glaciers melted and their gushing meltwaters narrowed, as the silt-laden winds were stilled and a drying sun bathed these lands, forests yielded to grasslands and the modern prairies first held dominion.

Iowa settlers of the 1800s may have guessed that gigantic animals had once trumpeted their deafening calls here, that elephantlike

mammoths and mastodons, beavers the size of bears, camels, lions, and giant armadillos had roamed Iowa's glacier-laden past. Perhaps the settlers found a mastodon tusk along the eroding banks of a creek, or plowed up a mammoth tooth that made their horses' molars look like toothpicks. Maybe when digging a well, they pulled up the cranium of a giant sloth. These great animals had been tracked by an earlier group of settlers—Iowa's first human immigrants, who arrived in North America on the tails of the last glaciers, when the cold pulled the earth's waters into frozen rank and the edges of oceans shriveled. Two-legged hunters then had leapt the islands of a land bridge stretching from Siberia to Alaska and started a methodical march south through the Americas. They crept into

Iowa about 12,000 years ago, their sharp-edged spears at the ready for hunting giant mammals.

At various times, the ice-age hunters' prey fed among short, patchy grasses that nestled near the glacial margins, or in parklands of

Living remnants of this era still cling to survival in northeastern Iowa, where balsam fir, Canada yew, and bearberry thrive in crevices and crannies that are cold and moist enough to meet these species' northern cravings. On nearby talus slopes,

may have understood that an even stranger past lay recorded beneath Iowa's glacial remnants. Life first surged and swayed here within the salty belly of shallow tropical seas. Our continent then clustered with other land masses near the equator. For hundreds of millions of years, life evolved within warm lapping waters, which receded only to advance again, now as a salty lagoon, now as a vast coastal swamp, now as the broad plain at the mouth of a great river. The remains of each passing environment sank to the watery floor, to be added to a thousand feet of rock-forming sediments, as if the life forms to follow would need the sure footing of a firm rock bed. Today, the slosh and gurgle of this ancient, watery Iowa can be sensed along rocky road cuts and riversides, which are exposed especially in Iowa's "Little Switzerland," the northeast corner of the state where glacial deposits are thinnest. Fossils of Iowa's earliest inhabitants—the crinoids and corals, trilobites and sponges, the steaming swampy forests of tree ferns—call out from the building stones, crushed rock, and coal mined from Iowa's depths.

spruce, or with dwellers of the arctic tundra. These cold-adapted communities followed the receding glaciers north, only to march south again with the next onslaught of ice. Their remains, pollen grains of the larch and fir, fossilized seeds and bits of wood, lie buried within peat bogs.

tiny Pleistocene land snails creep among golden saxifrage and northern monkshood, which are all now endangered species.

Iowa's successive waves of human settlers, on examining fossil-laden outcroppings of limestone and shale,

SUNRISE OVER FROZEN STORM LAKE, BUENA VISTA COUNTY

WATERFALLS OVER MOSSY
SANDSTONE, WOODMAN
HOLLOW STATE PRESERVE,
WEBSTER COUNTY

SANDSTONE OUTCROP
IN EVENING LIGHT,
LAKE RED ROCK,
MARION COUNTY

Clockwise from upper left: Bald eagle on the Des Moines River, Mahaska County; a wild rose, Iowa's state flower, Rock Rapids, Lyons County; bur oak, Madison County; Maquoketa Caves State Park, Jackson County

CLOCKWISE FROM UPPER LEFT: STORM BREWING OVER BENTON COUNTY; RED FOX PUP NEAR LIBERTY, CLARKE COUNTY; TASSELS AT SUNSET, CENTRAL IOWA; SYLVAN SCENE IN PIKES PEAK STATE PARK, CLAYTON COUNTY

ICE SHELVES
ALONG MIDDLE
MINERVA CREEK,
MARSHALL COUNTY

Wind, water, and ice: for millions of years they blew and ground and carved Iowa into the forms we see today, providing the substance and substrate for grasses, for prairies. But now the prairie has been broken, and the human hand has set out to transform the earth's shape. The land of water and ice and wind has been carved into terraced farmlands and leveled roadways, into cities and suburbs, into farmed wetlands, into straightened and dredged rivers. We have transmuted a land accustomed to growing seas of prairie into a fenced land of straight-rowed, domesticated grasses—as if the land and its wealth could be held within the dominion of the human fist.

Yet it was not always this way. The signs of earlier times lie everywhere, if one only knows where to look. These signs peek at us from roadsides as we speed by, they wink at us from riversides and waysides. The leavings of oceans and glaciers firm the ground beneath our feet. The remnants of prairie earth feed us. They live still, reminding us about the past and nurturing the present. They live still, tempting us to release our clutch just a bit, to reflood potholes and restore prairies, to return some of the land to its original inhabitants. Whispering to us to let the land go, to watch and see what returns. Witnessing to us what yet might come to be.

AN HONEST, HOPEFUL, HEROIC PEOPLE

By Mary Swander

Sunday, mid-morning in mid-January, the temperature 11 above zero, the wind gusty, blowing snow in swirls across the blacktop of an Iowa county road. I was driving cautiously, trying to ease my car toward an intersection, when suddenly my tires hit a patch of ice and I careened into the opposite lane. The car fishtailed, then with another powerful blast of wind, spun full-circle and went into the ditch, burying itself in a snowbank. Before I could even roll down the window or pry open my door, a farmer in brown coveralls and a red stocking cap stood beside me.

"Are you all right?" he called.

"Just a little shaken," I said.

"You're in there awful solid. I could never push you out. Do you have a chain?" I shook my head. Another man, who had stopped in his pickup, said he didn't have a chain, either. He flagged down still a third person who hopped out of his truck, hooked my vehicle to his, and with two or three yanks and tugs, metal buckling against metal, extricated me from the drift. While these three heroes disappeared down the road with a wave and a smile, I sat still for a moment and remembered how I'd experienced this kind of scene before.

Just a year and a half earlier, as I approached this same intersection, flood waters rising on both sides, I watched neighbor help neighbor row from their farmsteads in flatboats, rescuing each other from the devastation of the rushing currents. I inched back onto the icy road and realized how lucky I was to have these three men "just come along," with the honesty, know-how, and willingness to help me. That's why I like living in Iowa, I thought to myself. I like the people of this state.

THREE BROTHERS
READY TO PLANT
TREES NEAR
CUMMING,
WARREN COUNTY

A SAMPLING OF THE
MANY FACES OF
IOWA (THIS PAGE
AND FACING PAGE)

INSTRUMENTALISTS
IN A CIVIL WAR
REGIMENT FROM IOWA,
JOHNSON COUNTY

An F-16 fighter jet of the Iowa Air National Guard, Polk County

What is the special character that defines the Iowa people? Non-Iowans have plenty of stereotypes to offer. We've been painted pejoratively as the hayseed, the hick, the white-bread provincial, the dumb farmer. Since the political caucuses have thrust us into the media spotlight, our status has risen somewhat, to the level of the "average Joe American." Still, every four years or so, there's a move to pull the first caucuses out of Iowa and plant them in another state, one that would more accurately reflect the demographics of the whole nation.

We Iowans have internalized what we've been told. Often we devalue ourselves and buy the idea that we're a flat, boring people who live in a flat, boring landscape. Young college graduates still rush out of state to places where they think they'll find more opportunity and status. Those who stay learn to maneuver—often with humor—around the stereotypical images. A friend who is a successful graphic artist with her own business visits New York several times a year.

When asked her occupation, she cheerfully replies, "Hog farmer."

"That's what they're going to imagine, anyway," she laughs.

Back home, we may forget about our own heroes and heroines. We may know about Herbert Hoover, Iowa's native-born president, yet be unfamiliar with Carrie Chapman Catt, suffragette, peace activist, and founder of the League of Women Voters. We may study the drama of the Spirit Lake Massacre but never fully understand the agony of Chief Waubonsie's decision to send his Potawatomi tribe farther west, to Kansas. We may welcome Jesse Jackson to pose for a "photo op" milking a cow on an Iowa farm, but never know or comprehend the value of George Washington Carver's agricultural research at Iowa State University.

Gearing down further, we seldom stop to probe the character of those three hog farmers who may someday pull us all out of the ditch. What shaped their personalities? What created their link to me? To each other? To the rest of the world?

A YOUNG FARM
FAMILY AT HOME NEAR
SIOUX CENTER,
SIOUX COUNTY

ASSEMBLING A LINEAR
RECUMBENT BICYCLE
NEAR GUTTENBERG,
CLAYTON COUNTY

A NEW PAIR OF OVERALLS
FOR THE STATE FAIR,
POLK COUNTY,
EARLY 1970S

FISHING ON THE
RACCOON RIVER
NEAR LAKE CITY,
CALHOUN COUNTY,
1905

A PRIZE CATCH
FROM A FARM POND
NEAR CUMMING,
WARREN COUNTY

Surveying the
wreckage after a
tornado in
Muscatine County,
late 19th century

Cleaning up after
a tornado in
Manson,
Calhoun County,
July 1979

Even though Iowa is celebrating its 150th year of statehood, the state is still young on the national scale. Many families can tell vivid stories of their ancestors, just three or four generations back, who left the East, the South, or the Old Country and ventured into the vast unknowns of the prairie. What did they carry with them? Besides a Bible (or Book of Mormon, Torah, or Koran), plus a few tools and an heirloom or two, they carried in their wagons a sense of adventure, an ability to let go of the old and move on to the new. In their pockets, saddlebags, and knapsacks, they carried a ruggedness and a determination to survive.

Some of the Germans, Irish, Dutch, Swedes, Danes, African-Americans, and others who flooded Iowa during the middle and late 1800s came to escape poverty, conscription, slavery, or religious oppression. Most, however, were swept here by a sense of optimism and opportunity. The promise of cheap, fertile land lured many who had been persuaded by the press,

the railroad, or relatives that the West was a Garden of Eden.

"Wanted—thirty-seven thousand five hundred farmers!" read a headline in the *Waterloo Courier* in 1868. "Let the news be scattered. Let the home-hunting immigrant be informed that a free home awaits him in Iowa."

Once the sod was broken and the "free home" built, new Iowans did find themselves living on the richest soil on earth. But they also faced the realities of the state's climate and landscape. As soon as the pioneer settlers' crops of wheat, barley, and Indian corn popped out of the ground, some natural disaster waited to destroy them. Prairie fires, tornadoes, droughts, floods, and plagues of grasshoppers all had to be met with a sense of fortitude (either that or despair). The settlers' naive enthusiasm became tempered with an acceptance of hardship and the spinning wheels of fate. This temperance, in turn, fostered a plucky attitude toward life.

Scratch any Iowan and you'll

find someone who not only knows how to cope, but often copes with a sense of flair, eccentricity, or inventiveness. Open the door to an Iowa machine shed, and inside you may find a farmer tinkering over a work bench, tightening a few nuts and bolts to patch together an old milking machine, welding a new part for a combine, or inventing a water-powered tractor engine. Open the door to an Iowa home, and inside you may still find a crazy quilt in a frame, pieces of an old pair of brown coveralls and a red stocking cap sewn together to make a beautiful new creation. Iowans understand metamorphosis—the giving-way of the seasons, the giving-way of one substance, material, or idea into another—and they seem to give each other the time and space for transformations. Open the door to the character of an Iowan, and you may find the ghost of that pioneer on the prairie, picking up the pieces of a hog shed that had been ripped apart by a twister and using the lumber to build a new chicken coop.

PASSING OUT
BOTTLED WATER IN
DES MOINES,
POLK COUNTY, 1993
(NEAR RIGHT)

WORKING IN A
SOUP KITCHEN,
1935 (FAR RIGHT)

We still embrace difficulty with grace and even humor. "Iowa: A Place to Row," quipped the t-shirts (in a spoof on an old state motto, "A Place to Grow") during the 1993 flood. But underneath Iowa humor is compassion and a sense of the interconnectedness of society. In 1996, we may not be as conscious as our ancestors were of the strength of the whole chain. In 1846, Iowans knew they could not live without each other. They knew that their economy, their safety, their very lives depended on the help of family and neighbors. So the tight bonds of communities developed. So churches became not only religious but social centers. So a place such as Buxton, a mining town where African-Americans and Euro-Americans lived in integrated harmony, could thrive.

NATIONAL GUARD
TROOPS FILLING
SANDBAGS,
POLK COUNTY, 1993
(NEAR RIGHT)

IOWA HAS ONE OF
THE NATION'S MOST
EXTENSIVE, BEST
EQUIPPED HEALTH-
CARE NETWORKS
(FAR RIGHT)

An early 20th-
century barn-
raising near
Holy Cross,
Dubuque County

Today, although we are still a religious and bonded people, our formal institutions are larger and looser. Yet, once we are put to the test, our pioneer spirit kicks in and we hook into each other, bumper to bumper. Our heroics may be quieter now and not on such a grand scale as the pioneers', but they are nonetheless reminiscent. In 1859, Edwin and Barclay Coppoc of Springdale joined John Brown's abolitionist raid on Harpers Ferry; in 1991, Tom Harkin and Charles Grassley joined together to vote against the resolution to commence the Gulf War. Before the Civil War, our ancestors set up stations on the Underground Railroad; more recently, we set up hotlines to help farmers during the farm crisis and the drought of 1988. We set up Red Cross stations to help flood victims. We set up domestic-abuse centers to help battered women.

HASIDIC RABBI
AND SON (TOP);
AN IOWA BAPTISM,
POLK COUNTY,
1956 (MIDDLE);
POPE JOHN PAUL II AT
LIVING HISTORY FARMS,
POLK COUNTY,
1979 (BOTTOM)

"IOWA, YOU MAKE ME
SMILE:" A GALLERY OF
FRIENDS, SISTERS,
BROTHERS, AND COUPLES
(THIS PAGE AND
FACING PAGE)

LITTLE-LEAGUERS
LINE UP FOR THE
CAMERA IN
DES MOINES,
POLK COUNTY

At the same time, we are not a perfect people. The same problems that plague the rest of the nation plague us. We struggle to find ways to keep our environment clean but our economy moving ahead. We struggle to find the best ways to raise and educate our children. We struggle with issues of tolerance and differ-

ence. We struggle with crime, punishment, prisons, substance abuse, ignorance, and poverty. But the point is, we struggle and keep struggling, and keep hoping to find answers.

The people of Iowa have no major metropolitan area—at least, nothing as large as a Chicago or a Minneapolis—to set the tone. We have no major-league sports teams to create a sense of statewide camaraderie. Ethnically, we are a blend of northern-European cultures, with a sprinkling of African, Native, and Asian Americans. No single nationality predomi-

nates to give us a particular "face." By all rights, we should be a bland and loosely affiliated group. But anyone who moves here quickly comes to see that the people of Iowa have an unusual sense of self-identity.

IOWANS: A DIVERSE LOT (THIS PAGE AND FACING PAGE), WITH AN UNUSUALLY STRONG SENSE OF SELF-IDENTITY

BRIGHT FACES, BRIGHT
FUTURE: YOUNG
IOWANS OF THE PAST
AND PRESENT (THIS PAGE
AND FACING PAGE)

"This reminds me more of a small country than a state," a friend who moved to Iowa from the East Coast once told me.

Some say the state is unified because of its system of roads; others point to the fact that it has a strong, central newspaper. These superimposed structures help, but the common attitude of its people is the more intrinsic reason. Whether consciously or unconsciously, we place expectations on ourselves and

our neighbors that we will carry on in the founding spirit of hope, hard work, and pragmatism. As we do, we may spin out, get stuck, or discouraged, but at the core of our beings, we know that eventually we'll get back on the blacktop and be on our way.

PULLING OUT OF THE MUD, 1930S (ABOVE LEFT); RAGBRAI RIDERS PEDALING DOWN THE ROAD (FACING PAGE)

The family car
at home on
Des Moines' near
north side, 1949,
Polk County

A SOCIETY OF PURPOSE & ENERGY

By Craig Canine

 My family took long car-trips when I was a kid. We drove to the New York World's Fair, Washington, D.C., Niagara Falls, and one strangely subtropical Christmas, to San Diego. From the moment we left Iowa on our way to these destinations, spotting another car with Iowa plates was a big event. The minimum greeting was a wave; sometimes this would escalate to a friendly honk of the horn, or even a quick flash of the headlights. The farther away from home we got, the more exuberant these greetings became. It was as if every Iowa plate we encountered in a distant state belonged to a set of long-lost relatives. This was especially true if the Iowa plates happened to have the number 77 imprinted on the left-hand side, which meant that the car, like ours, was registered in Polk County. If we saw a Polk County car in, say, Virginia Beach, or near the Grand Canyon, we'd go crazy. We would do the wave, honk, and headlight flash, all three. A challenge arose when we saw an Iowa plate from a county other than number 77. What was county 65, 82, or 12? My father often knew the answer, but the real expert in this alphabetical code was my grandmother, who sometimes travelled with us. She knew them all, from 01 (Adair) to 99 (Wright). She had memorized Iowa's counties and their county seats when she was a student in a one-room schoolhouse, shortly after the turn of the century. Later, when she was a schoolteacher, she made sure that her pupils knew them, too. In those days, knowing the Iowa counties and their seats was considered no less impor-tant than knowing the states and their capitals.

Students in Iowa schools no longer memorize the counties. Perhaps because of this, county names are now spelled out on standard Iowa license plates. This removes an opportunity for trivia quizzes during car trips, I suppose, but it does not alter a larger fact: Iowans possess a strong, often enthusiastic sense of who they are and where they come from. Natives and longtime residents of the state seem to have that euphonious word *Iowa* stamped somewhere on their souls. "The state of Iowa," says writer Laurence Lafore, "is not a chunk of Midwest cut out by arbitrary lines from the enormous map of farmland that extends interminably through twelve states. It is a unit of consciousness, and it has a culture of its own. It exists in a way that Pennsylvania or New York do not. It is a state in the way that, say, Norway is a nation."

What accounts for this unique culture, this distinctively Iowan state of consciousness? It may arise from the view, widely if vaguely held both within Iowa's borders and without, that this is the quintessential state, the heartland's own heart. The story of Iowa is really the story of America—the tale of a

young, hopeful republic that, as historian Richard Hofstadter once put it, "was born in the country and moved to the city." Like the nation at large, Iowa began its official political life as a republic of small farmers and has gradually become more urban and industrial since its founding. Yet Iowa has remained more agrarian than the country as a whole, which is why people still look to the Hawkeye State as a fount of the old Jeffersonian virtues: independence, integrity, hard work, thrift, and pride of ownership. These values form the ideological bedrock upon which Iowa's 150 years of statehood have accumulated, like a deposit of fertile prairie loam.

Indeed, the last 150 years have seen a robust flowering of human enterprise on Iowa soil—farms, schools, industries, cities, towns, government, transportation systems, civic organizations, churches, recreational opportunities, the arts. Although none of these expressions of culture is unique to Iowa, there is a coherence here, a unifying core of values, that provides the state with its own singular sense of purpose and energy.

Iowa's culture (like everything else about the state) starts with the land, a fertile and inviting prairie situated in a beneficent climate between two great rivers. This is where the superlatives begin: Iowa has more prime agricultural soil than any other state. This single fact has nurtured and conditioned nearly all human activity on this plot of earth from the time of the last glaciers' retreat more than 10,000 years ago until the present.

In ancient times, the land now called Iowa sustained groups of paleo-Indians who foraged amidst plenty and hunted for big game, such as mastodons. Thousands of years later, the same land was home to mound-builders of the ancient Hopewell culture. These woodland peoples hunted and foraged along the Mississippi. Some scholars believe that members of this culture may have been the first people in what is now Iowa to practice agriculture. Subsistence, at any rate, came easily enough that these prehistoric Iowans had the leisure to create items that were not strictly necessary for survival. They crafted ornate items of jewelry, pottery, and metalwork.

The Hopewell culture disappeared mysteriously shortly after the time of Christ. But some of its characteristic activities, including moundbuilding and agriculture, continued during the habitation of succeeding woodland peoples. Between 900 and 1,000 A.D., these tribes created a most spectacular and enduring legacy from the land itself: They built large, leveelike mounds, sculpting earthen monuments in the shapes of 100-foot-long bears and birds. Now, a thousand years later, the results of their labors can be seen at Effigy Mounds National Monument in Allamakee County (I can still hear my grandmother saying, "County number three, Allamakee").

In June 1673, Jacques Marquette, a 36-year-old Jesuit missionary and explorer, was among a party of Europeans who paddled into view of the land now called Iowa. In his journal, Marquette wrote: "To the right is a chain of very high mountains, and to the left are beautiful lands." People who think Iowa is utterly flat might be interested to know that one of the first Europeans to lay eyes on the place remarked on its high mountains. (They weren't real mountains, of course, but river bluffs.)

On June 25, Marquette, along with a French-Canadian trader named Louis Joliet and five other *voyageurs*, landed on the west bank of the Mississippi and spotted human footprints. The footprints led to a trail. "We silently followed the narrow path," Marquette wrote, "and, after walking two leagues [about six miles], we discovered a village on the bank of a river." Historians think this was probably the Iowa River, near where it runs into the Mississippi.

AUTUMN ON THE
MISSOURI RIVER NEAR
COUNCIL BLUFFS,
POTTAWATTAMIE
COUNTY

CANOEISTS ON
THE UPPER IOWA
RIVER, ALLAMAKEE
COUNTY

WHETHER THE RESULT IS A GOLF COURSE (THIS PAGE) OR A SOYBEAN FIELD (FACING PAGE), THE HUMAN HAND HAS ETCHED PATTERNS OF USEFUL BEAUTY UPON IOWA'S GIFT OF GOOD LAND.

Harvesting ice near
New Hartford,
Butler County

"Then we heartily commended ourselves to God," continued Marquette, "and approached. I spoke to them first, and asked them who they were. They replied that they were Illinois; and, as a token of peace, they offered us their pipes to smoke."

After they met this welcoming group of natives, Marquette and Joliet caught their first glimpse of open prairie. It was like nothing they had seen before. "At first when we were told of these treeless lands," Marquette wrote, "I imagined that it was a country ravaged by fire, where the soil was so poor that it could produce nothing. But we have certainly observed the contrary; and no better soil can be found either for corn, or for vines, or for any other fruit whatever."

The first Europeans who took up residence in what is now Iowa were attracted not by rich soil, but by lead. A native woman, identified in some sources as the wife of Peosta, a Meskwaki warrior, is commonly credited with discovering lead ore in the "mountains" along the western

THE OLD SHOT
TOWER AND DUBUQUE
STAR BREWERY,
DUBUQUE COUNTY

bank of the Upper Mississippi. Native Americans and French adventurers mined these deposits, off and on, for a century.

In 1788, Julien Dubuque, an enterprising *voyageur* from Quebec, befriended the Meskwaki and received permission to mine lead on their lands. Dubuque and 10 companions paddled across the Mississippi and settled near Catfish Creek. They cleared several acres of river-bottom timber, built dwellings, put up fences, and planted corn. Near the deposits of galena ore that Dubuque called the "Mines of Spain," he and his companions built a furnace for smelting the ore into lead. This was the first example of European-style industry in the future Iowa. More lead mines and mining towns eventually sprang up. Before long, these were followed by large mills that sawed logs, which were floated down the Mississippi from Minnesota and Wisconsin, into lumber to supply the pioneers' insatiable demand as they settled Iowa in an energetic burst and then pushed on, ever westward.

A MODERN IOWA
DAIRY FARM,
WINNESHIEK COUNTY
(ABOVE); IN THE
HAYLOFT OF A TURN-OF-
THE-CENTURY BARN,
POLK COUNTY
(FACING PAGE)

In this swath of history—from about 1840 (before Iowa was yet a state) and extending backward far into the prehistoric past—lie the seeds of nearly all that Iowa has become. The Hopewell and other woodland cultures, the Ioway, and the Meskwaki (whom Europeans called the Fox) discovered and cultivated the land's richness. These native peoples bred and planted the corn that would become Iowa's, and the nation's, foremost crop. They lived lightly but well on the land—well enough to develop arts, crafts, music, dance, poetry, and monuments. Remnants of these early Iowa cultures survive today. The European settlers of the 19th century saw themselves as heirs to a New World. They were, however, only the latest in a long succession of peoples who found, on the ancient land now called Iowa, an inviting place to build homes, plant crops, and pursue refinements of culture.

From around 1840 onward, modern-day Iowa developed with

COUNTRY CHURCH
AND CEMETERY,
JASPER COUNTY

astonishing rapidity. The land between the rivers was surveyed, platted and divided into townships and sections—the rectangular gridwork that is, today, so strikingly evident when viewed from an airplane. Seemingly overnight, farms and towns germinated all over the gridwork, like weeds in a summer-plowed field. This settlement occurred in an explosive burst lasting, at its most intense, from the 1840s through the 1870s. In the midst of it, Iowa was admitted to the Union as the 29th state—the first free state to be carved out of the vast Louisiana Purchase. President James K. Polk signed the bill of statehood on December 28, 1846. The number of people living within Iowa's borders at the time was just under 100,000. Ten years later, the state's population had quintupled and stood at half a million. By 1900, census takers counted 2.2 million residents, not that far shy of the 2.8 million who live in Iowa today.

Patrol boys chat
with an officer in
Valley Junction,
Polk County,
1940

Bookmobile serving
rural Iowans,
1930s

Women in a water
taxi at Arnolds Park,
Dickinson County,
1942

BALLET IOWA
PERFORMANCE,
DES MOINES
CIVIC CENTER

REHEARSAL OF A VARIETY
SHOW TO BENEFIT
TRAER OPERA HOUSE,
TAMA COUNTY, 1949

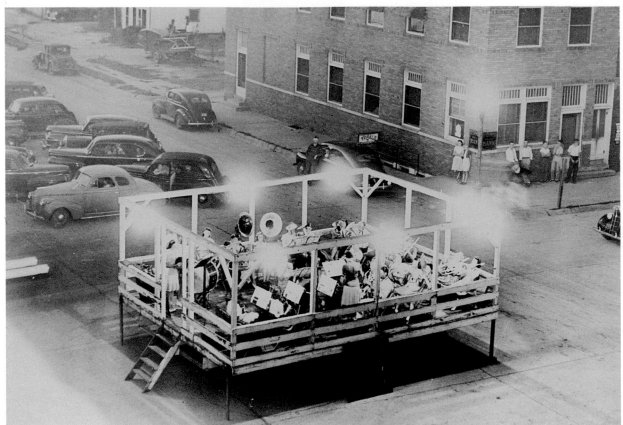

Town band
in Earlham,
Madison County,
1944

TWO RIVERS
FESTIVAL,
COURT AVENUE,
DES MOINES,
POLK COUNTY

III
—
101

GREAT COLONEL, A
PRIZE-WINNING
DUROC BOAR FROM
CRESTON, UNION
COUNTY, AT THE
IOWA STATE FAIR

Now, after a century and a half of statehood, Iowa can take stock of its place in the country and the world. Its most striking accomplishments still flow from its unparalleled endowment of rich soil. The marriage of good land and hard-working people has produced a litany of superlatives. Iowa is, for example, the most extensively cultivated state in the nation (some 92 percent of Iowa's 56,276 square-mile area is farmland). Though the number of farms in the state has been declining for some time, Iowa still has more than 30,000 farms with sales of at least $100,000—more farms in this category than any other state. In most years, Iowa is the nation's number-one producer of corn, soybeans, and red meat. It is the undisputed king of pork production: Iowa has twice as many hogs and pigs on farms as any other state and produces more than a quarter of the nation's pork. The total value of Iowa's crops in 1994 was more than $7 billion, second only to California.

A MODERN HOG-CON-
FINEMENT FACILITY IN
CENTRAL IOWA (ABOVE);
THREE LITTLE PIGS
(BELOW)

ICE CREAM
SHOP, FAIRFIELD,
JEFFERSON COUNTY

RECYCLING: A
GROWTH INDUSTRY
THROUGHOUT
THE STATE

BAKERY IN PELLA,
MARION COUNTY

Throughout Iowa's history, but especially within the past few decades, its people have cultivated far more than crops. Iowans are now harvesting the fruits of an increasingly diverse and resilient economic base. Manufacturing in the state now generates about three times as much personal income as does agriculture. Though Iowa ranks only 30th in population, it is the nation's 13th most productive manufacturing state. Machinery, processed foods, and electric and electronic components account for nearly half the total value of Iowa's manufactured products. Retail trade is a large and growing source of employment in the state. But the fastest-growing part of Iowa's economy is its service and professional sector, which now employs more people than either agriculture or manufacturing. Much of the growth in this category has occurred in insurance and financial services, especially in Des Moines. Iowa's capital city ranks second only to Hartford, Connecticut, as an insurance center.

CRAFTS FAIR AT
LAKE AHQUABI,
WARREN COUNTY

HATCHERY IN
WEBSTER CITY,
HAMILTON
COUNTY

HIGH-TECH
INDUSTRY IN IOWA:
THE LEGACY OF A
LONG TRADITION OF
INNOVATION AND
LEADERSHIP IN
APPLIED SCIENCE
AND TECHNOLOGY

MADE IN IOWA: FILMING
*THE BRIDGES OF MADISON
COUNTY* (ABOVE);
IOWANS AT WORK (FACING
PAGE AND BELOW)

CHEMISTRY LAB AT
DRAKE UNIVERSITY,
DES MOINES, ABOUT
1900 (BELOW);
A MODERN-DAY
CHEMISTRY CLASS AT
SIMPSON COLLEGE,
INDIANOLA (FACING PAGE)

III
—
110

Iowa stands out in education, too. It has among the lowest adult illiteracy and high-school dropout rates in the nation. Iowa students consistently rank at or near the top in college entrance exams. In spite of a long-standing trend toward school consolidation, the state has more than 400 public school districts. Iowa's public schools have acquired a nation-wide reputation for innovative teaching and administrative methods, curriculum reform, and financing. Iowa also has nearly 200 parochial and private schools, three state universities, more than 50 private colleges, and 15 community colleges. In short, the Hawkeye State is a good place to learn.

AMISH FATHERS
GUARD THEIR LOCAL
SCHOOL IN A 1965
CONTROVERSY OVER
TEACHER CERTIFICATION

School's out at
Hickory Grove
School, Lee County,
1948 (left); a mod-
ern Iowa kindergarten
scene (above)

AT THE IOWA GIRLS'
BASKETBALL STATE
TOURNAMENT

IOWA STUDENTS
GET AN EARLY START
IN LEARNING THE
KEYS TO THE FUTURE

STUDENTS ABOARD HACKS
AT THE CRAWFORDSVILLE
CONSOLIDATED SCHOOL,
WASHINGTON COUNTY,
1910

OLD MAIN,
DRAKE UNIVERSITY,
POLK COUNTY

THE UNIVERSITY OF
NORTHERN IOWA,
CEDAR FALLS, BLACK
HAWK COUNTY

A YOUNG VIOLINIST
REFLECTS IOWA'S
TRADITION OF EXCEL-
LENCE IN THE ARTS

A PENMANSHIP CLASS
FOR BOOKKFFPFRS AT
THE OLD HIGHLAND
PARK COLLEGE,
DES MOINES, 1899

A BUCOLIC PLACE TO
STUDY AT THE UNIVERSITY
OF IOWA, IOWA CITY,
JOHNSON COUNTY

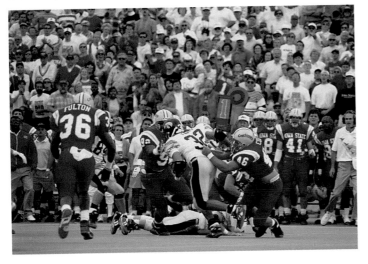

A CLASSIC ATHLETIC
RIVALRY: THE IOWA
HAWKEYES VS. THE
IOWA STATE
CYCLONES

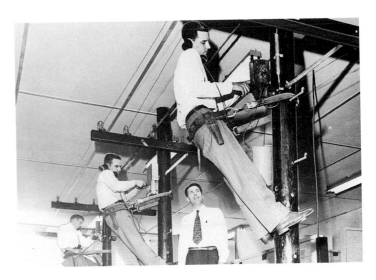

VOCATIONAL TRAINING
AT THE NORTHWESTERN
BELL BUILDING IN
DES MOINES, 1948

BY THE OLD BELL AT
SCATTERGOOD, A
QUAKER-RUN BOARDING
SCHOOL IN
CEDAR COUNTY

A MESKWAKI STUDENT
ADDS COLOR TO A
TRADITIONAL IMAGE,
TAMA COUNTY

Iowa's business and political leaders have devoted particular energy in the recent past to attracting more high-tech industries to the state. To some skeptics, the idea of a "Silicon Prairie" may seem as wildly optimistic as "Ski Iowa" posters. (Although even this tongue-in-cheek slogan isn't quite as far-fetched as it might seem; although Iowa doesn't claim to have any true mountain ranges, it does have eight commercial ski areas.) What skeptics may overlook, however, is that Iowa is no newcomer to the role of high-tech innovator. In fact, Iowans have led the world in developing some of the most important and definitive technologies of the 20th century—specifically the mechanical and genetic underpinnings of modern food production.

Nothing illustrates Iowa's historical inventiveness better than the development of the tractor and hybrid corn. Both of these cornerstones of modern agriculture were born and raised, to a large extent, in Iowa. They still provide the basis for some of the state's most important industries.

HAULING CORN TO THE CRIB NEAR STATE CENTER, MARSHALL COUNTY

III

119

SUNSET AT PLANTING TIME

YELLOWS AND GREENS
MAKE PATTERNS
ON THE LAND,
LEE COUNTY

An Iowan, John Froelich, built and operated the world's first working tractor in 1892. The word *tractor* had not yet been coined; the closest thing to it was "steam traction engine," a machine as large and ungainly as its name. Steam traction engines were railless locomotives—self-propelled steam engines, used mainly for plowing and threshing. Ordinary Corn Belt farmers couldn't afford such big, expensive rigs.

Froelich, like many farmers, loved to tinker in his shop. In addition to farming and black-smithing in Clayton County, he had a cus-tom-threshing business. In his shop, he equipped a wagon with a col-lapsible shelter that he and his threshing-crew members could live in when they were on the road—a precursor of today's mobile homes. To help tow all the equipment his crew trav-elled with, Froelich built another newfangled contraption. He mount-ed a Van Duzen gasoline engine (designed for stationary use) atop a heavy wooden frame equipped

with wheels. This hybrid machine could go forward or backward. Best of all, it had more horsepower than a steam engine that weighed nearly twice as much.

Froelich sold his invention in 1893 to a newly established firm called the Waterloo Gas Traction Engine Company. The company floundered at first. After the turn of the century, however, it became one of the strongest competitors in the

fledgling tractor industry. The company's Waterloo Boy One-Man Tractor was a top-seller during World War I, when shortages of human labor and draft animals on American farms encour-aged the adoption of labor-saving machines. Deere & Company bought the Waterloo Gasoline

HART-PARR
TRACTOR,
1913

Engine Company in 1918, in the midst of a postwar tractor boom. John Deere kept its tractor factory in Waterloo, where it grew and pros-pered. Today, Deere's Waterloo Works remains one of the world's leading centers of tractor production.

Froelich built the first mechani-cally successful tractor, but the first such machine to achieve commercial success was the creation of another Iowan, Charles Hart, and his friend Charles Parr. The two Charleses formed the Hart-Parr Gasoline Engine Company and built a factory in (where else?) Charles City, Iowa, in 1900. By 1903, Hart-Parr was turn-ing out more gas tractors than any other company, and it kept its lead for several years.

The Hart-Parr and Waterloo Boy factories were the keystones of a booming new Iowa industry. Between the turn of the century and the Great Depression, some 50 different tractor makers set up shop in the state.

THIS FARMER
PREFERS GREEN
MACHINES

THRESHING WITH STEAM
NEAR COLUMBUS
JUNCTION,
LOUISA COUNTY,
1894

A HALLOWEEN
HAY-BALE SCULPTURE,
NORTHWESTERN
IOWA

DEERE & COMPANY
TRACTOR WORKS
IN WATERLOO

A SWEET SIGN OF
LATE SUMMER IN
CENTRAL IOWA

The internal-combustion tractor revolutionized agriculture, dragging it into the modern age of oil, enamel paint, and down payments. Just as important to this revolution was the application of modern plant genetics to farming—for without higher-yielding crops, expensive machines such as tractors and combines wouldn't make sense, practically or economically. Corn was the first crop to be transformed by the new genetics. Here again, Iowa and Iowans played leading roles in the transformation.

Perry Greeley Holden, an academically trained botanist from Michigan, barnstormed through Iowa in so-called Corn Gospel Trains shortly after the turn of the century. As a faculty member of Iowa State College, Holden preached a "gospel" of better living through cultivating better types of corn. Another way he promoted this message among farmers was through corn shows. These events, which were tremendously popular from about 1910 to 1930, amounted to beauty contests for corn. Farmers would enter ten of their best ears in the shows, which were held during county fairs and other festivals.

III
—
128

CLOCKWISE FROM TOP LEFT ON
FACING PAGE: RENOWNED
BOTANIST GEORGE WASHING-
TON CARVER ATTENDED BOTH
SIMPSON COLLEGE AND IOWA
STATE COLLEGE; NATIVE SON
HERBERT HOOVER BECAME AN
INTERNATIONAL HUMANITARIAN
FIGURE AFTER SERVING AS U.S.
PRESIDENT; IOWA NATIVE AND
U. OF I. PROFESSOR JAMES VAN
ALLEN DISCOVERED EARTH-
ENCIRCLING RADIATION BELTS
THAT BEAR HIS NAME; RONALD
"DUTCH" REAGAN LAUNCHED
HIS PUBLIC CAREER AT WHO
RADIO IN DES MOINES.

Judges, many of them trained by Professor Holden, would rate the entries by appearance and award blue ribbons to the most uniform and shapely. The underlying assumption was that the best-looking corn was also the best-yielding.

A young Iowan named Henry A. Wallace challenged this assumption. Young Henry—son of Henry C. Wallace and grandson of "Uncle" Henry Wallace, editors of the well-known *Wallaces' Farmer*—performed a scientific yield test when he was only 16 years old. His test showed that there was no relationship between the appearance of an ear of corn and how well it yielded. Something deeper and far more complex than Professor Holden's corn-show standards was at work.

Young Henry learned what that "something" was when he was a student at Iowa State: It was the hereditary stuff of life called genes. Wallace became fascinated with the new science of genetics and incorporated its principles into his own experiments in corn breeding. Eventually, he produced a high-yielding hybrid (a cross between two genetically dissimilar strains of a plant), which he called Copper

Cross. In 1924, Copper Cross became the first hybrid ever to win the gold medal in the prestigious Iowa Corn Yield Contest at Iowa State. Wallace advertised Copper

Cross in a seed catalog and completely sold out. With the

HENRY A. WALLACE: PLANT BREEDER, U.S. SECRETARY OF AGRICULTURE, VICE PRESIDENT

belief that hybrids, as he wrote, "will eventually increase the corn production of the U.S. by millions of bushels," he founded the Hi-Bred Corn Company in 1926. Later, the word Pioneer was added to the name.

Wallace's rosiest predictions about the adoption of hybrid corn came true. In 1933, less than one percent of Iowa's corn acreage was planted with the new hybrid seed; only seven years later, in 1940, more than 90 percent of the Iowa corn crop consisted of hybrids. Today, that figure is virtually 100

percent, and Pioneer Hi-Bred International is the largest independent seed company in the world. Its success spawned a few hundred competing companies, many of them based in Iowa. The production of hybrid corn seed is now a major Iowa industry.

Iowa's contributions to technology continue today, and have branched out well beyond agriculture. The computer microchip and fax machine, for example, trace their development to discoveries that were made right here.

Yet it's the changes in agriculture that have had the greatest effect in Iowa. Developments in plant and animal genetics, mechanical engineering, and chemistry combined after the Great Depression to produce revolutionary changes in farming methods. These changes lie at the heart of the state's enormous agricultural productivity, yet many of the same innovations have contributed to problems such as chronically low farm prices, loss of topsoil to wind and water erosion, concerns about drinking-water quality, and the loss of farms due to the imperative (often heard since the 1950s) to "Get big or get out."

PREPARING A
SEEDBED WITH
HORSES (ABOVE)
AND PLANTING
IOWA'S BOUNTY
THE MODERN
WAY (RIGHT)

MESKWAKI
POWWOW,
TAMA COUNTY

AMANA
OCTOBERFEST,
IOWA COUNTY

BUCKSKIN
RENDEZVOUS,
VAN BUREN COUNTY

THE MIDWAY AT AN
IOWA COUNTY FAIR

IOWA LAOTIAN
DANCE TROUPE

ART IN THE PARK,
DES MOINES

But Iowans have proved remarkably adept at facing challenges and weathering storms—perhaps because farming itself is the creative management of vicissitude, and this skill has seeped into the culture at large. The hard times of the 1980s, in fact, brought forth a kind of creative renaissance in rural Iowa. Community theater groups were formed or revived; decrepit opera houses and movie palaces were restored; town squares got face lifts; high schools experienced surges of home-team spirit and support. Agriculture hit a low point, but cultural institutions that interpret and celebrate farming's proud past received infusions of energy and new blood.

Those institutions, which honor the hopeful, exuberant side of Iowa's agrarian heritage, have now emerged in the '90s strengthened and rejuvenated. The state is full of such places and events. For example:

❖ Living History Farms, near Des Moines, is the Colonial Williamsburg of American agriculture. It has few peers as a site for the accurate portrayal of the nation's agricultural past, from the times when Native Americans were Iowa's sole human inhabitants until the present.

IOWA SPECIAL
OLYMPICS IN AMES,
STORY COUNTY

HOBO CONVENTION
IN BRITT,
HANCOCK COUNTY

ANNUAL BEAVERDALE
CELEBRATION,
DES MOINES

JUST SAY NO DAY
IN CARLISLE,
WARREN COUNTY

SCANDINAVIAN
DAYS PARADE,
STORY CITY,
STORY COUNTY

LIVING HISTORY FARMS
1850S FARM,
POLK COUNTY

CIVIL WAR
REENACTMENT,
KEOKUK,
LEE COUNTY

OATMEAL DIVING AT
RIVERFEST, IOWA CITY,
JOHNSON COUNTY

NORDIC FEST,
DECORAH,
WINNESHIEK COUNTY

INDEPENDENCE DAY
PARADE IN SUMNER,
BREMER COUNTY,
1906

SCANDINAVIAN
DAYS PARADE,
STORY CITY,
STORY COUNTY

LADIES' SILVER BAND,
FORT MADISON,
LEE COUNTY,
1884

III

—

137

FOURTH-OF-JULY
FIREWORKS OVER
WEST OKOBOJI LAKE,
DICKINSON COUNTY

National Hot Air
Balloon Classic,
Indianola,
Warren County

A NEW, CHINESE-
MADE STEAM ENGINE
FOR THE BOONE
AND SCENIC VALLEY
RAILROAD,
BOONE COUNTY

DRAKE UNIVERSITY
CREW ON THE
DES MOINES RIVER,
POLK COUNTY

III
—
142

MEXICAN
CHILDREN'S FAIR,
DES MOINES,
1954

HIGH-SCHOOL
FOOTBALL GAME,
DES MOINES

THE FLOPPY SHOW,
WHO-TV STUDIO,
DES MOINES,
POLK COUNTY

STARTING LINE AT
THE DRAKE RELAYS
IN DES MOINES,
POLK COUNTY

DES MOINES
METRO OPERA,
SIMPSON COLLEGE,
WARREN COUNTY

❖ The Midwest Old Threshers Reunion, held each year during Labor Day weekend near Mount Pleasant, is a premier gathering of machines from the awesome age of steam on America's farms. An associated museum offers exhibits on themes such as the contributions of women to agriculture.

❖ The Annual Corn Husking Festival in Kimballton hearkens back to the days before World War II, when virtually all of America's primary crop was harvested by hand—and when hand-husking competitions were major spectator events in the Corn Belt.

SCOREBOARD FOR THE IOWA CORN HUSKING CHAMPIONSHIP, 1939

ATE CORN HUSKING CO

NET LOAD	PLACE	NO.	NAME	COUNTY	GROSS LOAD	GLEANINGS	HUSKS	Total DEDUCT.	NET LOAD	PLACE
2057.8	14	11	WOODROW DEITRICH	JASPER	2219	10.6	7.2	80.6	2138.4	12
2011.4	15	12	HENRY PETERSON	WEBSTER	2212	6.9	7.2	69.4	2142.6	11
2234.6	6	13	LEE STODGELL	LOUISA	2393	10.0	5.3	37.2	2355.8	3
1798.2	19	14	EARL JUSTICE	CRAWFORD	2019	10.7	9.2	116.9	1902.1	18
2389.3	2	15	ORVILLE RADKE	BUENA VISTA	2200	18.2	4.7	54.6	2145.4	10
2332.6	4	16	M.M. POMMER	BOONE	2299	27.0	6.7	120.1	2178.9	8
2149.5	9	17	CLYDE TEAGUE	SCOTT	2286	20.4		152.6	2133.4	13
330.4	5		...LE	DUBUQUE	2275	17.2		00.3	2184.7	7
	16		...RTS	MUSCATINE	25?4			04.5	24??	1
	17									

RUAN GREATER
DES MOINES
GRAND PRIX,
POLK COUNTY

A BIPLANE AND
AUTOMOBILE COMPETE
AT THE IOWA STATE
FAIR, POLK COUNTY,
1914

AT THE MIDWEST
OLD THRESHERS
REUNION,
MOUNT PLEASANT,
HENRY COUNTY

MEREDITH WILLSON
CONDUCTING THE
"IOWA FIGHT SONG"
AT A FOOTBALL GAME,
1963

BULLDOG BEAUTY
CONTEST AT THE
DRAKE RELAYS,
POLK COUNTY

❖ The Two-Cylinder Expo, held each year near Grundy Center, is one of the world's largest and most

impressive gatherings of nostalgia-inducing farm machinery (in this case, older John Deere tractors and equipment). Smaller gatherings of antique-tractor enthusiasts take place nearly every summer weekend somewhere in Iowa. Tractor pulls also attract thousands of fans throughout the state.

A FAN OF THE DES
MOINES SYMPHONY,
POLK COUNTY

❖ The annual rodeo in Sidney celebrates Iowa's historical role as a gateway to the Old West.

❖ Waverly, in the state's northeast quadrant, holds a large biannual sale of draft horses and horse-farming equipment, a vivid reminder of the days when "horse-power" referred to Belgians, Percherons, Shires, or mules.

ADMIRING THE BOUNTY
AT A DES MOINES
FARMERS' MARKET,
POLK COUNTY

GOING FOR A RINGER AT
THE IOWA STATE FAIR,
POLK COUNTY

III

149

SIDNEY RODEO,
FREMONT COUNTY

PELLA TULIP FESTIVAL,
MARION COUNTY

❖ And, of course, there's the end-of-summer institution known simply as "The Fair." Almost as old as the state itself, the Iowa State Fair each year draws hundreds of thousands of people—rural residents, townsfolk, and city dwellers alike—who wish to experience the sights, sounds, and smells of what is still, in essence, a king-size celebration of rural culture.

STATE FAIR EXPOSITION
BUILDING AND
SURROUNDING
EXHIBITS,
POLK COUNTY,
ABOUT 1912 (LEFT);
THE FAIR TODAY
(ABOVE)

WAITING FOR
THRILL-SEEKERS

FINE
SHOWMANSHIP

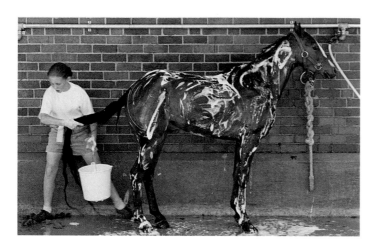

SCRUBBED FROM
TIP TO TAIL

BLUE-RIBBON
POTATOES IN THE
HORTICULTURE
BUILDING

NATIVE AMERICANS
AT THE STATE FAIR,
ABOUT 1900

PRIZE-WINNING PIES

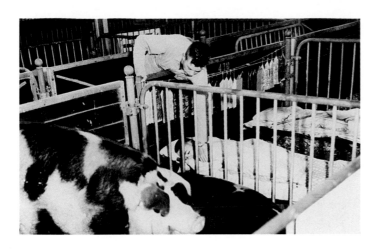

IN THE SWINE
BARN, 1957

AN AWARD-
WINNING EWE AT
THE STATE FAIR

A WINNING
PERFORMANCE IN
THE RIDING ARENA

SERVICE WITH
A SMILE

ON THE MIDWAY

CHAMPION
BABY BEEF,
1938

PICNIC AREA IN
WINTER, NORTHWEST
IOWA (LEFT); SUMMER
PICNIC NEAR
DES MOINES,
POLK COUNTY
(ABOVE)

Simply to classify Iowa as a rural state, however, would be misleading. Most of the state's residents live neither in the rural countryside nor in cities, but in small towns. The Iowa Department of Transportation, which prepares the official state highway map, reports more than 900 "cities and villages" within the state's borders. Few states—even those that cover a far larger area than Iowa—have more surviving towns. Only about 70 of Iowa's incorporated communities have populations greater than 5,000. The remaining 800-some dots on the state map rank somewhere in size between Muckersville (pop. 6) and Hiawatha (pop. 4,986). These stalwart little towns, unassuming and often unheralded, harbor the true strength and character of Iowa. Most natives of the state who have achieved national prominence have hailed from this great reservoir of all-American pride and gumption.

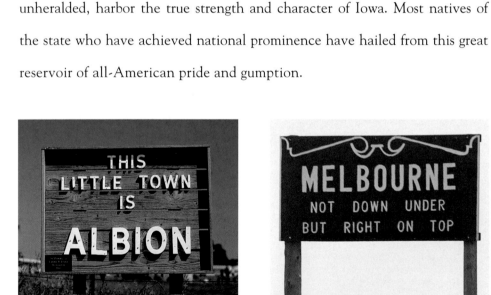

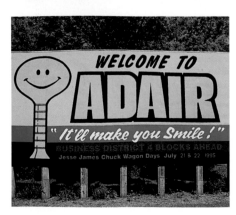

CANDY-COLORED
BIKES AT A FAVORITE
STOP IN WILTON,
MUSCATINE COUNTY

Taking a break
from festivities
at the Meskwaki
Settlement,
Tama County

HERBERT HOOVER BIRTHPLACE,
WEST BRANCH, CEDAR
COUNTY (TOP); MAMIE DOUD
EISENHOWER BIRTHPLACE,
BOONE, BOONE COUNTY
(ABOVE LEFT); JOHN WAYNE
BIRTHPLACE, WINTERSET,
MADISON COUNTY
(ABOVE RIGHT)

Here are a few famous natives of small-town Iowa: Johnny Carson (television personality), Corning; the Everly Brothers (musicians), Shenandoah; Bob Feller (baseball player), Van Meter; George Gallup (opinion pollster), Jefferson; James Norman Hall (coauthor of *Mutiny on the Bounty*), Colfax; Herbert Hoover (U.S. President), West Branch; John L. Lewis (labor leader), Lucas; Glenn Miller (big-band leader), Clarinda; the Ringling Brothers (circus founders), McGregor; Wallace Stegner (Pulitzer Prize-winning novelist), Lake Mills; Donna Reed (actress), Denison; Ruth Suckow (novelist), Hawarden; Billy Sunday (baseball player, evangelist), Nevada; James Van Allen (physicist), Mount Pleasant; Henry A. Wallace (corn geneticist, U.S. Secretary of Agriculture, Vice President), Orient; Henry C. Wallace (editor, U.S. Secretary of Agriculture), Catalpa; John Wayne (actor), Winterset; Andy Williams (musician), Wall Lake; Grant Wood (artist), Anamosa.

Bring those who were born on Iowa farms and in Iowa cities into the picture, and the list of famous natives expands to include: Leon "Bix" Beiderbecke (jazz musician), Davenport; Norman Borlaug (Nobel Prize-winning botanist), near Protivin; Lee DeForest (inventor), Council Bluffs; Mamie Doud Eisenhower (first lady), Boone; Paul Engle (poet), near Cedar Rapids; Simon Estes (opera singer), Centerville; Art Farmer (jazz musician), Council Bluffs; Esther Pauline Friedman (columnist known as Ann Landers), Sioux City; Pauline Esther Friedman (columnist known as Abigail Van Buren), Sioux City; Susan Glaspell (author and dramatist), Davenport; Lou Henry Hoover (first lady), Waterloo; Cloris Leachman (actress), Des Moines; Aldo Leopold (forester and ecologist), Burlington; Jerry Mathers (TV star of *Leave It to Beaver*), Sioux City; Harriet Nelson (TV costar of *Ozzie and Harriet*), Des Moines; Meredith Willson (Broadway composer and lyricist), Mason City.

"UNCLE" HENRY WALLACE
HOUSE, DES MOINES (TOP);
AMERICAN GOTHIC HOUSE
IN ELDON, WAPELLO
COUNTY (MIDDLE);
HERBERT QUICK SCHOOL-
HOUSE IN GRUNDY CENTER,
GRUNDY COUNTY (BOTTOM)

The cities of Iowa are linked closely, in space and spirit, with their predominantly agrarian surroundings. There isn't an office building in the state located more than 15 minutes' drive from a soybean field. Yet Iowa does have places that are undeniably urban, and so it shares with the nation as a whole both the challenges and the rewards of an increasingly urban culture.

Iowa's eight municipalities with populations greater than 50,000 are distributed with unusual evenness across the state. Council Bluffs and Sioux City look to the West from the Missouri River; Des Moines, Cedar Rapids, Waterloo and Iowa City are scattered across the state's broad interior; and Dubuque and Davenport are situated on the Mississippi, at the top and bottom of what writer Phil Stong humorously called Iowa's "hearty and not unbecoming pot-belly to the east."

On the next tier down in size, with populations of 25,000 or more, Iowa boasts another cavalcade of fine towns with distinguished pasts and promising futures. They are Fort Dodge, Ames, Mason City, Marshalltown, West Des Moines, Cedar Falls, Clinton, Bettendorf, and Burlington. (Ottumwa misses this boat, according to the 1990 census figures, by a mere 500 people—the population, that is, of a Bussey or a Beacon, an Orleans or a Richland.)

In a small town, everyone knows the mayor. No citizen is more than one degree of separation, by personal acquaintance or blood relation, from the town council. This situation tends to produce an electorate that is curious and well informed. Because Iowa is a culture of small towns, it's no wonder that the electorate of the state as a whole is civically alert and engaged. Interest in politics and public affairs runs deep, as a visit to most any small-town cafe, salon, or barber shop will confirm. Opinions flow as freely as morning coffee. What comes as a surprise to many outsiders—media people, for example, who flock to the state during the Iowa caucuses—is how open-minded and progressive most of those opinions are.

A BRIDGE OVER THE
CEDAR RIVER IN CEDAR
RAPIDS, LINN COUNTY
(ABOVE); BARGES PLY
THE MISSISSIPPI RIVER,
NORTHEASTERN IOWA
(FACING PAGE)

Iowa has always been a progressive state, in the sense that its citizens have consistently embraced change when they've perceived it as change for the better. This tendency goes back to the Civil War, when Iowans were overwhelmingly opposed to slavery. A handful of the most committed abolitionists acted as conductors on the underground railroad, which crossed the southern half of the state. Iowa was ahead of the nation as a whole in enacting civil rights laws. It was also quick to enact a prohibition law (1884) and was one of the first states to adopt direct primaries (1907).

In agriculture, Iowa was a leader in the Patrons of Husbandry move-ment, known as the Grange. This organization was superseded after the turn of the century by a variety of farmers' groups, including the Farmers Union, the National Farmers Organization, the National Farmers Holiday Association, and the American Farm Bureau. Most of these national farm groups were either founded in, or derived their top leaders from, Iowa. Milo Reno, Edwin T. Meredith, James Howard, Oren Lee Staley, the three Henry Wallaces, Seaman Knapp, "Tama Jim" Wilson, and Dixon Terry are only a few of the many farm leaders with strong ties to Iowa who have achieved prominence in the nation and the world.

No discussion of Iowa's progressive past would be complete without mention of Carrie Lane Chapman Catt. Born in Wisconsin, she moved with her family to Floyd County, near Charles City. The only woman in her class at Iowa State, she was also class valedictorian. In the 1880s, she became increasingly active in the women's suffrage movement, first in Iowa and then as a national leader. She was president of the National Woman Suffrage Association when, in 1919, Congress passed the 19th Amend-ment giving women the right to vote. Then Catt became the head of a new group, the League of Women Voters. Only within recent years has she begun to receive her due as a historical figure of international sig-nificance. Her childhood home near Charles City is being restored, and a building at Iowa State University was recently renamed and dedicated in her honor.

CARRIE CHAPMAN CATT HALL, IOWA STATE UNIVERSITY (NEAR RIGHT); UNDERGROUND RAILROAD STATION IN SPRINGDALE, CEDAR COUNTY (FAR RIGHT)

WOMEN'S CONGRESS TENT AT THE IOWA STATE FAIR, 1899 (NEAR RIGHT); CIVIL RIGHTS MARCHERS (FAR RIGHT)

PEACE MARCH AT THE STATE CAPITOL, 1986 (NEAR RIGHT); KIDS DEMONSTRATE FOR FARM SAFETY IN DES MOINES, POLK COUNTY (FAR RIGHT)

MAIN STAIRWAY IN THE
OLD CAPITOL, IOWA CITY
(ABOVE); IOWA STATE
CAPITOL ROTUNDA,
DES MOINES (FACING PAGE)

SPRING AT THE
STATE CAPITOL
BUILDING,
POLK COUNTY

OLD MILL ON
TURKEY RIVER,
ELKADER,
CLAYTON COUNTY

DES MOINES
ART CENTER
RICHARD MEIER
ADDITION,
POLK COUNTY

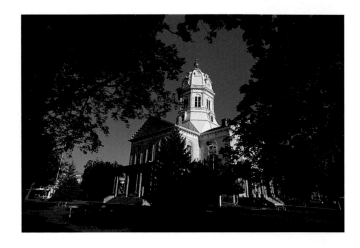

THE COURTHOUSE,
WINTERSET,
MADISON COUNTY

ABBIE GARDNER'S
CABIN, ARNOLDS
PARK, DICKINSON
COUNTY

BRUCEMORE
MANSION,
CEDAR RAPIDS,
LINN COUNTY

STATE HISTORICAL
SOCIETY BUILDING,
POLK COUNTY

BIG CANOE CHURCH,
DECORAH,
WINNESHIEK COUNTY

BEARDSHEAR HALL,
IOWA STATE UNIVERSITY .

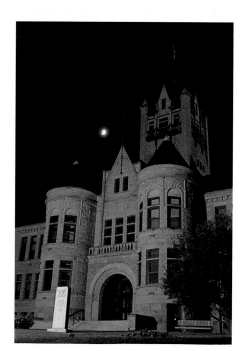

TERRACE HILL, IOWA'S
OFFICIAL GOVERNOR'S
RESIDENCE, POLK COUNTY

JOHNSON COUNTY
COURTHOUSE,
IOWA CITY

NATIONAL BALLOON
MUSEUM, INDIANOLA,
WARREN COUNTY

This revival of interest in Carrie Chapman Catt exemplifies the spirit of purpose and energy that will serve Iowa well in its future— a spirit that recognizes the past, finds inspiring strengths there, then builds upon those strengths as we move confidently forward. A lifetime ago, Iowa ranked first in farm-owned automobiles and in per-capita ownership of telephones and radios. Today, Iowa has the most extensive fiber-optic communications network in the world. Tomorrow, who knows? I only hope that when Iowans see each other on the high-tech highways of the future, they wave.

THE ENDURING PROMISE OF IOWA: WALKING BEANS

By Michael Martone

"Would you like to walk beans this weekend?" my friend Thayer Brown asked me one July day. I accepted his invitation on the strength of that turn of phrase, "walking beans." It conjured up, in my mind, a visual pun in which I was leading a bunch of legumes around by a leash—a notion I couldn't shake, even when Mr. Brown explained the actual procedure. And that procedure sounded inviting as well, patrolling along the rows of beans with family and neighbors and then hoeing out the weeds we found there—cockleburs, sunflowers, burning bush, devil's shoestrings, and the volunteer corn sprouting from seeds spilled last year when the field had been planted to corn. Early the following Saturday morning, I drove to the Brown farm. It's located near Turin, in the western part of the state. I joined a group of Browns and their neighbors, who gathered at the edge of a soybean field on bottom land near the Little Sioux River. Thayer Brown's pickup raced out of the hills toward us along the section road. He brought us the new implements we were to use while walking beans that day. These implements looked a little like traditional hoes. They were not made of wood and metal, however, but of white plastic pipe. A loop of nylon rope dangled from one end of each pipe. Mr. Brown poured a brand-new liquid herbicide into the hollow handles. The chemical filled the handles and ran down to the rope-wicks and saturated them. He capped off the open end of one handle and handed me my "hoe."

A FORWARD-LOOKING FARMER IN A STRIP-CROPPED FIELD NEAR ALTA VISTA, CHICKASAW COUNTY

A PANORAMIC
VIEW OF RIPENING
SOYBEANS NEAR
ANKENY,
POLK COUNTY

Walking beans this year would mean travelling the rows and painting weed-leaves with a lick of the wick. We had to avoid the beans, because they were also susceptible to the chemical's herbicidal action. This was new. The herbicide was supposed to be absorbed into the vascular system of the touched plant, the poison drawn down into its very roots. In a week or so, the weed would be dead.

My purpose in bringing up this moment is not to discuss the merits and detriments of certain technologies. It is to point out the moment when a future arrived in Iowa. Other futures, I assume, arrive daily. What interests me about this particular moment is how it was met. Iowans, it seems to me, are particularly adept at negotiating the meeting of the past and future, at negotiating the transformations of yesterdays into

tomorrows. We were about to engage in a classic Iowa summer ritual, yet in a way that was radically new. We even called our newfangled implements "hoes." We talked as we walked and touched the weeds with our wands, the talk connecting me to past summers on the farm, just as the bushy eruptions of volunteer corn hearkened back to events in this field the previous summer. With our new tool, we continued to work.

Iowa's roads and railways (and central location) have made the state a national crossroads, meeting place, and transportation hub

We know the world and the things in it by sorting those things into categories: plants and animals, city and country, Iowans and non-Iowans. That day walking beans, we made the distinction between the leaves of the soybean plant and those of the weeds. But such categories are not always hard and fast. Last year's corn was a crop, but in this year's bean field, it's a weed. Boundaries between the groupings shift in response to the appearance of things new and—well, different, like our novel "hoes." In response, we can expand our categories of perception, or we can create new categories altogether. Either approach demands an act of imagination, a creative impulse to entertain new ways of ordering and reordering the world.

Iowans have this ability, this willingness to suspend conventional groupings and to entertain the possibilities of other arrangements. It's perhaps their greatest asset as they meet the future, day by day.

Here's an example to illustrate this flexibility of vision, this suppleness in meeting and accommodating the future. Iowans used to say that, no matter where you were in the state, you were no more than ten miles from a railroad. As the state's extensive railway system has contracted during this century, Iowans have responded in a creative way: They have converted many of the abandoned right-of-ways into one of the most extensive networks of bike trails and hiking paths in the country. There is a practical logic at work in this creativity. Using these abandoned stretches as linear public parks keeps the corridors preserved and alive. They're a boon to recreation and exercise, but they're also a hedge. Who knows when the economic winds will shift again, and it might make sense once more to lay track?

The writer Hamlin Garland called Iowa "the Middle Border." On one level, we sense that somewhere within the borders of Iowa, the East ends and the West begins. The Middle Border also implies that Iowa is the setting for transformation and change, even while it embraces stability and order. The Middle Border (like all borders) divides even while it connects.

Look at the road map of the state and read it as an expression of both of these functions of borders. There is no other state in the Union where the grid of roads and country lanes so closely matches the original boundaries of township surveys. The pattern of expanding rectangles begins with quarter-section farm fields, then jumps to include the sections bounded by roads and highways. Sections are the building blocks of townships. These townships are stacked row upon row to make counties, and the counties are laid out tier by tier—nine neat ranks of them, lined up from top to bottom of the state. Iowa is a patchwork of patchworks. This pattern of grids within grids is the ultimate expression of being bounded, enclosed, defined.

And yet, at the same time, the very coordinates that demarcate one square mile from the next—the roads themselves—are also corridors of transmission. Roads aren't walls; though they separate and divvy up the land, they serve to communicate between and connect all the parcels. The whole setup functions as a huge vascular system that saturates each bounded cell of soil with effortless access and egress. Look at that map again and imagine it as a picture of a vibrant, 99-celled organism. The cells are differentiated and unique, each one contributing in its own way to make up and sustain that wondrously ordered living system called Iowa.

Here's another example of what I mean—another of Iowa's creative responses to shifting boundaries of time and place. The original townships, a highly imaginative invention of their time, always included a concession of land to support free public schools. Consolidations of those original school districts, however, have forced Iowans to rethink the very idea of the classroom. The result is that the state has embraced a vision of a virtual schoolhouse constructed of satellite dishes, fiber-optic cable networks, and computers. Any part of the organism will be able to tap into expertise and resources of information from any other part.

The experience of living in such a place is thrilling, though subtle. It involves cultivating the ability to shift between ways of looking at things, the ability to shift gears between hoe and "hoe," from schoolhouse to "schoolhouse." Iowans daily flex this metaphorical muscle. They get the jokes. They envision puns ("walking beans," for example). They shoot the breeze. They shake out the rug. These are creative and healthy activities. Such vision allows Iowans to escape the tyranny of the literal, and to confront the new and unexpected with a habit of mind that questions habitual thought and practice.

It is no mistake, I think, that *Field of Dreams* is one of the most telling of our cultural icons. Author W. P. Kinsella's original story incorporates, in its main character, this Iowan knack of seeing when the character imagines his farm as a baseball field. Perhaps even more telling is the actual existence of such a field. Created for the movie version of the book, the imagined set has taken on a life of its own. Near Dyersville is a monument to the Iowan habit of mind: A humble baseball diamond represents the space that is made for living and working amidst the dreaming.

A BOY'S OWN
FIELD OF DREAMS,
WINNESHEIK COUNTY

SNOW TUBING,
PALO ALTO COUNTY

EMMETSBURG
WINTERFEST,
PALO ALTO COUNTY

CROSS-COUNTRY
SKIING,
DUBUQUE COUNTY

CHAIR LIFT AT
MT. CRESCENT
SKI AREA,
POTTAWATTAMIE
COUNTY

SWIMMERS ON
LAKE OKOBOJI,
DICKINSON COUNTY

REGATTA AT
RATHBUN LAKE,
APPANOOSE
COUNTY

SWIMMING HOLE
NEAR GLENWOOD,
MILLS COUNTY

SOCCER PLAYERS IN
IOWA CITY,
JOHNSON COUNTY

Consider for a moment those times in our history when some of our actual borders really did get up and move. I'm not speaking metaphorically now—I'm thinking of the recent summer of floods when Iowa's bordering rivers and their tributaries quite literally left their beds and took a walk. It amounted to a physical rearrangement of the entire state. The native response to the daily disasters was remarkable. There was patience, persistence, good humor, and courage. The floods were surprising in their voraciousness and in their scale, but Iowans were not taken by surprise. Rivers had come to life amidst a population expert in dealing creatively with shifting boundaries, skilled in coping with new ways of ordering and reordering the world.

THE FLOODWATERS OF 1993 ERASED BOUNDARIES AND CREATED NEW BARRIERS IN CITY AND COUNTRY ALIKE, POLK COUNTY (LEFT, TOP AND BOTTOM)

BICYCLISTS AND
PEDESTRIANS IN ROYAL,
CLAY COUNTY
(LEFT); SHOPPING
DISTRICT IN MARION,
LINN COUNTY
(BELOW, TOP); A WILD
ROSE, THE STATE
FLOWER, IN BLOOM
(BELOW, BOTTOM)

IV
—
189

In the summer of 1994, I returned to the Brown field near Turin. I wanted to show my six-year-old son the farm where, 10 years before he was born, I walked beans. The Browns no longer walk beans. They drill them now, allowing the dense crop canopy to shade out the weeds. Mr. Brown sat my son on his shoulders and waded out, knee deep, into the green sea of soybeans. The summer before, this same field was submerged beneath the green water of the Little Sioux River. I wanted my son to see this place and meet these people. I am hoping that a habit of thinking and acting will rub off. I hope that he can learn to see the metaphorical connections between an ocean and a farm field. I'm hoping he will come to realize that this suppleness of thought is a special gift.

Now, my son and Mr. Brown turn and call to me as I stand on the shore. I am looking out, trying to catch a glimpse of the breaking waves, the next future moment.

CONTRIBUTING PHOTOGRAPHERS:

Steve Alexander
Page 99A

Jervas Baldwin
Pages 10, 76A

Tom Baldwin
Pages 158K, 159A, 159B, 159G, 159H, 159I, 159M

Rob Beeston
Pages 67C, 72B, 79E, 135C, 135H, 158B, 158I, 159J, 159L, 173E

Mark Bendixen
Page 76B

Craig Canine
Pages 163A, 175D

Lisa Cannon Blumhagen
Pages 5A, 13B

Matt Bradley
Pages 79I, 88, 182-183

David Cavagnaro
Pages 30-31, 53, 54H, 91, 135I, 173B

George Ceolla
Cover, pages 7, 35, 42, 52, 54I, 55C, 61, 72D, 73C, 77B, 78C, 104A, 107A, 112-113, 132, 138-139, 169F, 180B

Bob Coyle
Page 170

Jim Day
Pages 15B, 123, 134A, 134B, 134C, 134D, 135E, 135G, 137A, 161, 162A, 162C, 185B, 185D

Nancy Ferguson
Page 143B

French Studios
Pages 167, 189A

Michel Friang
Pages 13A, 135B

Julie Ann Glauberg
Page 71A

GYZINIWA
Pages 12A, 12B, 55E, 55H, 78D, 78G, 101, 108B, 134F, 148C, 149A, 153B, 154C, 155C, 155D, 155E, 169E

Ric Johnson
Pages 79A, 146, 158C, 159C, 159D, 159E, 159N

Barbara Kashian
Pages 54G, 135A

Mike Kregness
Pages 4C, 66, 67A, 103B, 108A, 158D, 158G, 158H, 159K, 163C, 180A

Bill Kuhn
Pages 54A, 55G, 78A, 78I, 108D, 109C, 116D, 116F, 125A, 143A, 164, 172C, 191D

Carl Kurtz
Pages 22, 24, 25, 28, 44-45, 46, 47, 50, 189B

Joan Liffring-Zug
Page 172F

Andy Lyons
Pages 55F, 115, 154B, 172D, 175C, 190E

Curt Maas
Pages 6, 18-19, 20, 21A, 63, 64B, 73D, 118, 180F, 190C, 190G, 190H, 191C, 191E, 191I

Ric MacRae
Pages 23, 37, 48D, 79F, 133, 172B, 180D, 190F

Steve Ohrn
Pages 158E, 159F, 163B, 172E

Sherry Pardee
Pages 54F, 78E, 117F, 158A, 158F, 159O

Craig Perman
Page 141

Ila Plasencia
Pages 72C, 78H

Kay Prall
Pages 171, 173F, 177

Ken Regan, Camera 5
Page 109A

Lynda Richards
Pages 8-9, 54C, 54D, 78F, 79D, 126-127, 135D, 135F, 151, 172A, 180C, 191A

John Schultz
Pages 5B, 14A, 55D, 77A, 79B, 104C, 108C, 111, 120-121, 134E, 143C, 148A, 149B, 154D

Scott Sinklier
Pages 59, 74-75, 78B, 90, 107A, 174, 175B, 186A, 186B, 190A, 190I, 191B, 191H

Ty Smedes
Pages 21B, 29A, 29B, 29C, 32, 33, 48A, 49B, 142C, 190D

Perry Struse
Pages 49A, 49D, 55A, 79H, 95, 97, 105A, 119B, 128, 149C, 150, 162B, 166, 173A, 173C, 180E, 185A, 190B, 191F, 191G

David Thoreson
Pages 43, 81, 89, 94-95, 124B, 137C, 142A, 156-157, 165, 176, 188

Will Van Overbeek
Pages 11, 79G

Archie Webb
Page 140

Michael Whye
Pages 4A, 4B, 5C, 26-27, 40-41, 48B, 48C, 49C, 54B, 60, 87, 104B, 105B, 109B, 154A, 160, 173D, 178-179, 184D, 185C

Ryan Zelinsky
Page 155B

PHOTOS COURTESY OF:

Jervas Baldwin
Pages 84-85 (select images)

Blue Cross/Blue Shield of Iowa
Page 67D

Robert Boldridge
Page 72A

Helen Melaas Canine
Page 82

Suzanne Conyers
Pages 71B, 98A

David and Geraldine Cross
Pages 13C, 73A, 76C

Deere & Company
Page 125B

Des Moines Register
(photo by Gary Fandel)
Page 12C

Jean Wallace Douglas
Page 130

Dubuque Area Chamber of Commerce,
(photo by Design Photography, Inc.)
Page 93

General Growth Corporation
Page 109D

Paul Hoxsie
Pages 84-85 (select images)

Iowa Air National Guard, 132nd Fighter Wing (photo by Tech. Sergeant Dave Wilson)
Page 57

Iowa Department of Economic Development
Pages 17, 106B, 116B, 184B, 184C

Iowa Department of Transportation
Pages 84-85 (select images)

Iowa Division of Tourism
Pages 3, 154F, 157B, 175A, 184A

Iowa Girls High School Athletic Union (photo by John Overton)
Page 116A

Iowa Sesquicentennial Commission
Pages 84-85 (select images)

Iowa State University
Pages 117C, 169A

Iowa State University, Special Collections
Pages 16, 98B

Joan Liffring-Zug Collection, State Historical Society of Iowa— Iowa City
Page 14B

Robert Morris
Page 54E

National Pork Producers Council
Page 103A

Pioneer Hybrid International, Inc.
Page 106A

State Historical Society of Iowa —Des Moines
Pages 15A, 38, 55I, 62, 67B, 71C, 83, 96, 98C, 99B, 100A, 110, 117A, 117D, 117E, 122, 129A, 129B, 131, 137B, 142B, 146-147, 148B, 152-153, 154E, 155A, 155F, 158J, 169B, 169C

State Historical Society of Iowa —Iowa City
Pages 55B, 56, 64A, 73B, 129C, 136, 169D

University of Iowa
(photo by Tom Jorgensen) Page 117B
(photo by Jim Richardson) Page 129D

University of Northern Iowa
Page 116E

Wallaces Farmer
Pages 34, 68-69, 79C, 80, 92, 102, 114, 116C, 119A, 124A, 144-145

Special thanks to Loren Horton, State of Iowa Historian

BON BENTON BLACK HAWK BOONE BREMER

ROLL CASS CEDAR CERRO GORDO CHEROKEE

CRAWFORD DALLAS DAVIS DECATUR DELAWARE

E FLOYD FRANKLIN FREMONT GREENE GRUNDY

HENRY HOWARD HUMBOLDT IDA IOWA JACKSON

UTH LEE LINN LOUISA LUCAS LYON MADISON

MONONA MONROE MONTGOMERY MUSCATINE

POCAHONTAS POLK POTTAWATTAMIE POWESHIEK

A TAYLOR UNION VAN BUREN WAPELLO WARREN

NNESHIEK WOODBURY WORTH WRIGHT ADAIR

TON BLACK HAWK BOONE BREMER BUCHANAN

CEDAR CERRO GORDO CHEROKEE CHICKASAW

DALLAS DAVIS DECATUR DELAWARE DES MOINES

FRANKLIN FREMONT GREENE GRUNDY GUTHRIE

HOWARD HUMBOLDT IDA IOWA JACKSON JASPER

LINN LOUISA LUCAS LYON MADISON MAHASKA

MONROE MONTGOMERY MUSCATINE O'BRIEN

AS POLK POTTAWATTAMIE POWESHIEK RINGGOLD

AYLOR UNION VAN BUREN WAPELLO WARREN

WINNESHIEK WOODBURY WORTH WRIGHT

ADAIR ADAMS ALLAMAKEE APPANOOSE AUDU
BUCHANAN BUENA VISTA BUTLER CALHOUN C
CHICKASAW CLARKE CLAY CLAYTON CLINTON
DES MOINES DICKINSON DUBUQUE EMMET FAYET
GUTHRIE HAMILTON HANCOCK HARDIN HARRISON
JASPER JEFFERSON JOHNSON JONES KEOKUK KO
MAHASKA MARION MARSHALL MILLS MITCHELL
O'BRIEN OSCEOLA PAGE PALO ALTO PLYMOUTH
RINGGOLD SAC SCOTT SHELBY SIOUX STORY TA
WASHINGTON WAYNE WEBSTER WINNEBAGO W
ADAMS ALLAMAKEE APPANOOSE AUDUBON BEI
BUENA VISTA BUTLER CALHOUN CARROLL CAS
CLARKE CLAY CLAYTON CLINTON CRAWFORD
DICKINSON DUBUQUE EMMET FAYETTE FLOYD
HAMILTON HANCOCK HARDIN HARRISON HENRY
JEFFERSON JOHNSON JONES KEOKUK KOSSUTH L
MARION MARSHALL MILLS MITCHELL MONON
OSCEOLA PAGE PALO ALTO PLYMOUTH POCAHON
SAC SCOTT SHELBY SIOUX STORY TAMA
WASHINGTON WAYNE WEBSTER WINNEBAGO